Transforming
Body and Soul

Transforming Body and Soul

Therapeutic Wisdom in the Gospel Healing Stories

Steven A. Galipeau

Paulist Press

New York 🕊 *Mahwah*

Library of Congress Cataloging-in-Publication Data

Galipeau, Steven A.
    Transforming body and soul: therapeutic wisdom in the Gospel healing stories / by Steven A. Galipeau.
        p.   cm.
    Includes bibliographical references.
    ISBN 0-8091-0442-3
    1. Spiritual healing—Psychology   2. Spiritual healing—Biblical teaching.   3. Jesus Christ—Miracles.   4. Bible N. T. Gospels—Psychology.   I. Title.
    BT732.5.G34   1990
    226.7'06—dc20   90-36421
                                                                        CIP

Published by Paulist Press
997 Macarthur Boulevard
Mahwah, New Jersey 07430

Printed and bound in the
United States of America

Contents

Dedicated to my wife,

Tia

JUNG AND SPIRITUALITY

The *Jung and Spirituality* series provides a forum for the critical inter-action between Jungian psychology and living spiritual traditions. The series serves two important goals.

The first goal is: *To enhance a creative exploration of the contributions and criticisms which Jung's psychology can offer to religion.* Jungian thought has far-reaching implications for the understanding and practice of spirituality. Interest in these implications continues to expand in both Christian and non-Christian religious communities. People are increasingly aware of the depth and insight which a Jungian perspective adds to the human experi-ences of the sacred. And yet the use of Jungian psychoanalysis clearly does not eliminate the need for careful philosophical, theological and ethical reflection or for maintaining one's centeredness in a spiritual tradition.

Thus the second goal is: *To bring creative insights and critical tools of religious studies and practice to bear on Jungian thought.* Many volumes in the *Jung and Spirituality* series work to define the borders of the Jungian and spiritual traditions, to bring the spiritual dimensions of Jung's work into relief, and to deepen those dimensions. We believe that an important outcome of the Jung-Spirituality dialogue is greater cooperation of psychol-ogy and spirituality. Such cooperation will move us ahead in the formation of a postmodern spirituality, equal to the challenges of the twenty-first century.

Robert L. Moore
Series Editor

Daniel J. Meckel
Managing Editor

Preface

Many people have contributed to the development of this book. Morton Kelsey introduced me to the psychology of C.G. Jung and the possibility of reconnecting to our religious traditions through the living psychic reality of the unconscious. John Sanford's many books have been most influential, especially his studies of the teachings of Jesus and other biblical material. Glenn Foy has been a companion for many years in the search for healing in my own life.

Those who have consulted me as a psychotherapist over the past eighteen years have helped me more deeply appreciate the struggles of the human soul and the unfolding of the healing process. Terri Shelton and Caryl Porter supported my work in the early chapters and made helpful suggestions. My wife Tia listened to the entire text and made many important comments. The sections with stories about the healing of women were much improved with her assistance. John Sanford also read parts of the manuscript and offered suggestions for clarification.

Rusty Miller assisted greatly with the editing of the text. Many points are clearer and unnecessary repetition avoided because of his work. Mary Beth Gaik typed the manuscript into its final form.

*"I wound and I heal;
and there is none that can deliver out of my hand."*
                                        Deuteronomy 32:39

Introduction

It is easy to find literature on Christianity and healing. Surprisingly, little of it explores the actual accounts of the healings of Jesus, and none examines their psychological aspects. My goal in this book is to examine the psychological dimensions of the gospel healing stories and to discover ways we can apply them to our own lives.

For Christians, faith in Jesus generally focuses on his death and resurrection. This is certainly fitting. The gospels indicate, however, that Jesus' healing and teaching ministries are also important. Today the teaching has received valuable attention; scholars and pastors have thoroughly explored the parables.[1] Not so the healing stories. While there is renewed interest in healing, little has been done to relate it to the healing of Jesus. While there were other teachers in those times, no one could heal in Jesus' extraordinary way. When John the Baptist's disciples came to question him, Jesus offered his healing work as a sign of his special call from God (Mt 11:2-6; Lk 7:18-23).

This is not a book about spiritual healing.[2] Rather, it emerges from modern experience in psychotherapy and pastoral counseling. The approach is primarily psychological but very much in keeping with the gospel healing stories. Rich in psychological and symbolic content, these stories strongly complement the teachings of Jesus. More than mere incidents of people being mysteriously healed, the healings of Jesus substantiate his teachings, just as the teachings extend the meaning of the healing. Together they are the rock on which the resurrection is built.

In the gospel healing stories lie possibilities for a healing ministry much more profound than modern Christianity has generally recognized. Jesus' healings have much in common with modern depth psychology. They express the deepest meaning of incarnation—that God was fully present in the person of Jesus and healed through him as well as raising him from the dead, as he would wish to do through any properly centered human being. God asks us all to be channels of healing. The gospel record offers us a vision of the potential for healing today.

1

NOTES

[1] John A. Sanford's *The Kingdom Within: The Inner Meaning of Jesus' Sayings* is an excellent study of the teachings of Jesus from a psychological point of view. Norman Perrin's *Rediscovering the Teachings of Jesus* and Joachim Jeremias' *The Parables of Jesus* are noteworthy books by scholars.

[2] Christianity should be grateful to those like the late Agnes Sanford who have kept this aspect of Christian healing alive. Her many books are a good introduction to this area of healing. In *Christianity and Healing*, Morton T. Kelsey gives a good overview of the healing that has lived in the history of Christianity.

Chapter 1
Jesus as Healer

What kind of healer was Jesus? A close look at the gospel healing stories reveals an assortment of techniques and healing methods unusual to people of modern times, especially those who view healing through the medical model our society favors. Jesus does not heal as we would assume. Some of his methods are even repulsive. They don't fit in with modern sensibilities. During the remarkable development of medical science we have lost sight of other, equally important forms of healing. We need all the resources available today to break down our preconceptions about healing, especially the healing work of Jesus. These resources have not been available in past centuries. Before looking at the healing stories it is important to establish an overall impression of Jesus as a healer.

Consider the healing of the blind man in Mark 8:22-26. One of the curious things Jesus does is to spit on the man's eyes. While modern medicine might tell us that saliva can be a good lubricant for the eye, no medical practitioner would spit in the eye of a patient to facilitate a cure. Elsewhere in the gospel of Mark, in the story of the healing of a deaf man with a speech impediment, Jesus spat and touched the man's tongue (Mk 7:31-37). A similar action taken by Jesus to bring about healing of another blind man is found in the gospel of John. We are told that "he spat on the ground and made clay of the spittle and anointed the man's eyes with clay" (Jn 9:6). Whether we like it or not, such actions are integral parts of the healing of Jesus.

The healing stories make clear that Jesus was not a medical doctor. Those who seek his healing do not approach him as a physician. In one story, about a woman with a flow of blood, we hear that the woman had "suffered under" many physicians before she searches for Jesus (Mk 5:25-34). Jesus does not criticize the work of physicians, but offers a very different and specifically religious approach. He carried no medical tools, performed no surgery, administered no drugs.

Jesus' strange techniques and healing methods would also seem unusual to practitioners of traditional Christian spiritual healing. Very little in modern Christian healing resembles what Jesus is said to have done in the gospels. Like the modern doctor, no Christian healer would spit in a person's eye. He would pray for divine intervention and lay on hands. Jesus, however, does very little praying for healing and seldom lays on hands.

We can be grateful to the evangelists for recording the healing of Jesus as well as they did, for they had nothing in their own experience to relate it to. Very little healing took place in the Old Testament and in the Israelite religion, and nothing to compare with the healings of Jesus could be found in the Mediterranean world of that time. The evangelists recognized Jesus' work as unique and presented it as such. Today we can review and seek to understand these acts as the four evangelists could not. Our perspective is enlarged by the contributions of modern anthropology, depth psychology, and psychosomatic medicine.

Anthropologists who study primitive cultures and religions from around the world report that many primitive peoples have a religious healer: the shaman or medicine man. A number of such cultures are alive today. In our own country some native American tribes still have shamans who do healing work—not as physicians or doctors, but with a unique religious approach.

Only recently have western people begun to reverse their devaluation of primitive people, their tendency to disparage primitive religions and rationalize away the healing work of the shaman. "Primitives" were viewed as totally undeveloped: What could they know about healing? For example, when the anthropologists first went into the field, they would interview the natives, asking questions like: "Where do babies come from?" A typical native response was "They come from the gods." The first anthropologists laughed at such stupidity. Later anthropologists began to realize that the first generation had judged the so-called primitive people too fast. They interviewed more carefully, and in doing so they discovered that primitive people realized that babies are born only after sexual intercourse. "Then why do you say that they come from the gods?" the anthropologists would ask. "Because," the natives would reply, "intercourse does not guarantee that there will be a child. There is always an unknown factor involved which is the work of the gods."

By improving their interview techniques, anthropologists have learned that in many respects primitive people are extremely well developed.[1] One such area is the healing work of the shamans, which in an extraordinary way parallels the healing of Jesus. Indeed, from the standpoint of healing, Jesus can be viewed as a highly developed shaman.

Westerners have difficulty grasping the shamanistic viewpoint. If it was challenging for anthropologists to understand primitive thinking, it is even harder for a medically oriented mind to do so. Where a doctor generally approaches illness *concretely,* in terms of body functioning, the shaman does so *symbolically,* in terms of what the parts of the body and the illness mean spiritually. We have already seen this in connection with the role of saliva. Doctors generally do not ascribe much healing value, if any, to spit. In our culture it is considered repulsive. In parts of the gospels, too, it has a repulsive aspect. For example, in the passion narratives of Mark and Matthew we hear of Jesus being spit on by his accusers (Mk 14:65; Mt 26:67). By contrast, the three healing stories involving saliva indicate that it also has a healing quality. In some primitive cultures saliva has a profound symbolic meaning: it represents the essence of a person. Among certain African tribes it is customary for individuals to rise in the morning, spit into each palm, and raise the palms to the sun as an offering of the individual self to God. The use of saliva in healing would indicate the involvement of the full substance of the healer. Jesus' use of it carries this same symbolic value and indicates his involvement in the healing process.

A shaman would not only look at things like saliva differently from a medical man; he would have his own view of the world. While we in the west live primarily in a world of externals where scientific-objective methods form the normal approach to life, shamans inhabit an inner spiritual world filled with forces that can bring illness or healing to human beings. Guided by older, experienced mentors, shamans experience this inner realm over an extended time.

In our century we find a view of reality similar to shamanism in the extraordinary work of C.G. Jung. Jung carries Freud's concept of the personal unconscious to much deeper levels, describing how we also experience what he calls a collective unconscious, a vast inner world we share with all people. This world contains patterns of experience—called *archetypes* by Jung—that affect all people's lives.[2] For Jung, psychological health requires that a person adapt not only to the outer world, so important to all other treatment modes, but to the inner world as well. The person who lives only in the outer world is, for Jung, as sick as the schizophrenic who has become completely overwhelmed by the inner world.[3] Life as Jung saw it calls us to come to grips with both. The inner world is the more crucial because there, amid all that might be impinging upon our personalities, we can find the inner center of the personality, which Jung called the Self. Within each person is a wisdom greater than that of the ego, a wisdom that would shape and mold the personality to become more whole, to fulfill its full potential, and to find healing.[4]

This view of life has many parallels to the gospels.[5] Jesus spoke of the kingdom within, an inner world with which we must wrestle to establish the rule of God in our lives. In his healings Jesus drives out demons and works with spirits. To modern people this is a strange way of healing, but for a shaman it is not. Jesus' teachings and healings testify to an inner world, crucial to a healing ministry and to the spiritual life. The early church fathers held a similar view, but for a variety of reasons it has almost disappeared in western thought.[6]

A crucial ingredient of shamanism is ecstatic experience, usually centered in dreams and visions. Such experiences carry the shaman into the inner world to confront its mysteries and be shaped into the person he is called to become. In Jung's psychology and its practice, the same experiences are central: through dreams and other manifestations of the unconscious, a person can be guided into relationship with his own inner center. Likewise, John Sanford and Morton Kelsey have written of the importance of dreams in the Christian tradition, beginning with biblical times and continuing into the days of the early church.[7] The gospels present ecstatic experiences in the life of Jesus: his baptism, his wilderness experience, his transfiguration. His teaching and healing also express a deep affinity with the inner world.

Keeping in close touch with the inner realm obliges the shaman to spend time alone. In some primitive communities the shaman lives apart from the rest of the tribe just for this purpose. Young men or women who show signs of having a shaman's gifts are set apart so that their gifts can mature. According to the gospels, after times of great healing or teaching, Jesus withdrew to find his own inner center, the voice of the Father. Luke often shows Jesus withdrawing, especially when people sought to bestow earthly power on him. Jesus likened such actions to the temptations he had undergone from Satan in the wilderness.

We know little, if anything, of the life of Jesus before his baptism. Since the earliest age given for the beginning of his ministry is thirty, he probably spent many long years exploring his inner world. Scholars like to look for early influences on his life and teaching. Very likely he conversed with those like John the Baptist, who also had prophetic-shamanistic personalities. The shaman's greatest instruction, however, comes from within, from his tutelary spirits;[8] to these he is ultimately responsible. It was to God, his deepest inner voice, that Jesus directly responded and was responsible.

Another area in which the ministry of Jesus parallels shamanism is the dramatic phenomenon of weather intervention. The gospels, for example, report the stilling of the storm, when the disciples are filled with awe (Mk 4:35–41; Mt 8:23–27; Lk 8:22–25). Jesus acts in order to save their lives. Because of his deep relationship to the inner spiritual world, he is able to act in the midst of a life-threatening event of nature. Jesus' action implies a close relationship between nature and the world of the spirit. The same sort of relationship appears in accounts of shamans who intervene in the weather to save life and in other ways to preserve the natural order. One such case from earlier in this century involved a Navajo medicine man named Hosteen Klah. A white woman friend of his witnessed the event with a number of other people.

Traveling across the Arizona desert on a blustery, cloudy day, their group encountered a cyclone heading straight for them. They were filled with terror and panic. As they rushed to get back into their car, Klah began walking toward the whirling mass. Along the way he picked up bits of earth and desert plants and put them in his mouth while he chanted. Suddenly he held up both hands, and raised his voice in a loud chant. After a moment the column divided in the center, the upper part rising into the clouds and the lower half spinning off at a right angle to its former course. Later, asked about the plants and soil he had picked up, Klah said, "The Spirit of the Earth is more powerful than the Wind Spirit."[9]

Shamans have a close relationship to the earth, the source of all their drums, pipes, rattles, and other healing tools. They are astute observers of nature and of plants and animals. Jesus likewise derives strength and wisdom from the natural world. As we have seen, he did not hesitate to use a substance like saliva in his healing. His teachings have a particularly earthy quality to them. He teaches using images, not concepts, and most of the images come from nature and daily life: the mustard seed, the sower, the birds of the air, the lilies of the field. Jesus speaks of vineyards, bread, wedding feasts, weeds, nets, and sheep. In comparison Paul and the other New Testament authors use very few images from nature.

Though Jesus often withdrew to be alone with God and the inner world, he was not an ascetic like John the Baptist. John led a spartan existence, wearing coarse clothing and fasting in the wilderness. Jesus was very much at home in the wilderness, but he also spent a good deal of time in the cities and towns with people, often enjoying food and wine with others. The gospels contrast him to John in this regard (Mt 11:18–19; Lk

7:33–34). Jesus fasted to seek a vision or inner experience much as shamans do, not as a regular lifestyle. He wore no unusual clothing, neither
the coarse garments of John nor the formal attire of the scribes and the
Pharisees.

The shaman's call to know the inner world and mediate it to others
often comes through personal illness.[10] An initiatory illness begins the
spiritual journey. The shaman is intimately involved in his own healing
process, beginning his training as one who needs to experience directly the
healing power of the spirits.[11] In this case there is no direct parallel with
Jesus, no significant illness early on. Illness, however, is not the only call to
be a shamanistic healer. "The spirits" draw a person to the inner world to
understand its healing mysteries.[12] No matter how Jesus was called by
God, he knew first-hand, as all shamans must, the pain and suffering of
human life.

The shaman's call is very different from that of the medical doctor.
Experiencing one's own need for healing is not necessary to study medicine. Nor does the doctor have to experience medicine as a patient, and
dissect his own body. The shaman, on the other hand, must become inwardly dismembered and reborn.[13] In the process of losing an old personality to discover a new one, he encounters the spiritual forces that impinge
on human life. The shaman must learn through personal experience which
of these forces are truly healing and life-supporting and which are
destructive.

Shamanistic healing and the medical approach are not mutually exclusive, though there is a danger of getting so caught up in one that we miss
the value of the other. In our culture we risk being so attached to the
medical model that we do not see the other side. Fortunately, today some
physicians are moving toward greater balance. Albert Schweitzer, for example, remarked, "Some of my steadiest customers are referred to me by
witch doctors. Don't expect me to be too critical of them."[14] Schweitzer
found that the African shaman knew quite well when illnesses were psychological or psychogenic, and when they were substantially physical; the
shaman would refer the latter cases to the medical clinic. On our own
Indian reservations the value of the shamans has become more recognized;
medicine men are given rooms in the hospitals on the Navajo reservation
so that they can take part in total health care.[15]

The positive attitude of Christianity toward healing has provided fer-
tile ground for the development of medical science. Ironically, this is not
the form of healing Jesus practiced. Seeing his healing ministry in the

context of shamanism can help us integrate its principles into the practice of the healing arts.

NOTES

[1] See Laurens van der Post's *The Heart of the Hunter.* This book on the bushman of South Africa is an excellent presentation of the nearly lost wisdom of a so-called primitive people.

[2] See C.G. Jung, *The Archetypes and the Collective Unconscious, Collected Works,* Vol. 9i, pp. 3–41.

[3] See C.G. Jung, *Modern Man in Search of a Soul,* Chapters 6 (especially p. 120), 9, and 10.

[4] John A. Sanford, *Healing and Wholeness,* Chapter 5, "Healing in the Psychology of C.G. Jung."

[5] John A. Sanford, *The Kingdom Within.*

[6] See Morton T. Kelsey, *Encounter with God,* for a discussion of what happened to this view of reality from the viewpoint of western philosophy and theology.

[7] John A. Sanford, *Dreams: God's Forgotten Language* and *Dreams and Healing.* Morton T. Kelsey, *God, Dreams, and Revelation.*

[8] Mircea Eliade, *Shamanism: Archaic Techniques of Ecstasy,* Chapter 3.

[9] Franc Newcomb, *Hosteen Klah: Navajo Medicine Man and Sand Painter,* Chapter 16, pp. 198–200.

[10] Eliade, Chapter 2.

[11] John G. Niehardt's *Black Elk Speaks,* pp. 20–50, has a good example of this type of call to be a shaman.

[12] See Lyall Watson's *Lightning Bird* for a dramatic account of how the "spirits" of Africa initiated an Englishman into these mysteries of life.

[13] Eliade, Chapter 2.

[14] Norman Cousins, *The Anatomy of an Illness,* p. 68.

[15] See Donald Sandner's *Navajo Symbols of Healing.*

Chapter 2
Healing and the Evangelists

Modern research shows that if a number of people witness the same event, such as an accident, each one will notice different things and give seemingly conflicting reports. People experience life in different ways and have different ways of reporting their experiences.

The healing stories concerning Jesus are recorded in four different gospels. A close look at these gospels reveals that each of the authors has his own approach to the material. Each has his own view of Jesus, and each writes at a different time in the life of the early church. Before exploring the gospel healing stories, it will be helpful to look at the different approaches of the evangelists. It is important to realize that there are different versions of the same stories, and to evaluate which of the accounts of the evangelists describes most accurately the healing work of Jesus.

Modern biblical scholars offer us a basic outline of the way the gospels came to be written. When Jesus died, about 33 A.D., the church continued as a branch of Judaism. The early Christians continued to practice the Jewish faith and their new faith alongside one another. The teachings of Jesus, his healing ministry, and the other events of his life were passed on orally. Segments of teachings or other events may have been written down, but not in the form in which we have them today. The first gospel, the gospel of Mark, was not recorded until about 70 A.D. At this time the temple in Jerusalem was destroyed and any group linked to temple Judaism was forced to reorganize its religious life. Mark's contribution was to gather available oral and written information about Jesus and put it together. Later, possibly around 80 A.D., Matthew did the same. Matthew copied most of the gospel of Mark and added teaching material available to him that was not found in Mark. Matthew also added a birth narrative and accounts of the post-resurrection appearances. Luke was the next to formulate his gospel. Like Matthew, he copied most of the gospel of Mark and included, in a different format, some of the same teaching material that Matthew added in his gospel. Luke also added other teaching material and healing stories not found in either Matthew or Mark. Luke tells a different birth account than Matthew and more post-resurrection accounts.

John was the last evangelist to write. His gospel is quite different from the other three. Some scholars like to say that John's gospel contains the teaching of the risen Christ rather than the teaching of the earthly Jesus. To the early church these were of equal significance. There is little overlap between the gospel of John and the "synoptic" gospels of Mark, Matthew, and Luke. John tells the fewest healing stories, but his are longer. In his unique way he covers many of the points brought forth in the stories found in the synoptics. As we move into a discussion of the various healing themes, we will see John's special contribution to the gospel healing tradition.[1]

The majority of the healing stories are found in the three synoptic gospels. Usually each tells the same basic story, but with subtle and important differences. Mark, as we shall see, is often the closest to the actual healing work of Jesus. Matthew and Luke tend to alter the healing stories to fit "their" picture of Jesus. The record of healing suffers in the process. An example appears in Mark 6:1–6a and the parallel passages in Matthew 13:53–58 and Luke 4:16–30. This is the Markan text:

> He went away from there and came to his own country; and his disciples followed him. And on the sabbath he began to teach in the synagogue; and many who heard him were astonished, saying, "Where did this man get all this? What is the wisdom given to him? What mighty works are wrought by his hands! Is not this the carpenter, the son of Mary and brother of James and Joses and Judas and Simon, and are not his sisters here with us?" And they took offense at him. And Jesus said to them, "A prophet is not without honor, except in his own country, and among his own kin, and in his own home." And he *could* do no mighty work there, except that he laid his hands upon a few sick people and healed them. And he marveled because of their unbelief (Mk 6:1–6a, author's italics).[2]

Up to this point in Mark's gospel, Jesus is an extraordinary teacher and healer, with great wisdom and the capacity to facilitate transformation of body and soul. Now we hear from Mark that he comes to his own country, the place in which he grew up. He encounters people who knew him as a younger man. When they hear his teaching and see his "mighty works" they are amazed: How can such things come from the carpenter they had known? They take offense—recognizing his gifts, but unable to see him in a new way. They cannot accept the fact that he had grown and developed and become closely linked with God. Because of their attitude, Mark reports, Jesus *could* do no mighty works there. With the type of

attitude he encountered, the closed minds, the preconceptions, it was impossible for Jesus to accomplish much healing. Without the proper attitude, these people could not receive what Jesus had to offer.

The situation in this story is often repeated today. Returning to visit
their families, individuals often find themselves seen as they were when
they last lived at home. Old family patterns recur that make it difficult for
them to be different. To continue their growth and development, such
individuals must live their lives in new and more open situations. What
Jesus experienced is really not unusual. It is hard for us as human beings to
see people differently after we have known them in a certain way.

Mark's indication that Jesus *could* do no mighty works is another
common and frustrating human dynamic. Jesus could not do much healing
with these people because of their closed attitude. Today, if a person does
not have faith in a doctor, the doctor's ability to assist him can become
limited. Faith in the healer is an important dynamic of modern medical
treatment.[3] Modern research on the placebo effect makes this clear.[4] Likewise, in psychotherapy, the attitude of the patient is essential to the pro-
gress of the therapy. Faced with a certain level of resistance, no therapist,
no doctor—not even a healer like Jesus—will succeed. As we will see, it is in
those who can make a change of attitude that healing of both body and
soul occurs. Mark's account stresses the importance of having the right
attitude for both healing and the spiritual life. His point is reiterated in
other healing stories.

Let us now turn to the versions of the same story in Matthew and
Luke. Matthew's version reads as follows:

> And when Jesus had finished these parables, he went away from
> there, and coming to his own country he taught them in their
> synagogue, so that they were astonished, and said, "Where did
> this man get this wisdom and these works? Is not this the car-
> penter's son? Is not his mother called Mary? And are not his
> brothers James and Joseph and Simon and Judas? And are not all
> his sisters with us? Where then did this man get all this?" And
> they took offense at him. But Jesus said to them, "A prophet is
> not without honor except in his own country and in his own
> house." And he *did* not do many mighty works there, because of
> their unbelief (Mt 13:53–58, author's italics).

Down to its last sentence, the passage from Matthew closely resembles the one from Mark. Jesus comes to his home town, and those who had

known him earlier do not accept his wisdom and spiritual abilities. The final sentence, however, has been changed dramatically with only the slightest alteration in the phrasing. Instead of indicating like Mark that Jesus "*could* do no mighty work there," Matthew says that he "*did* not do many mighty works." The Markan story presents what happened as the direct result of the attitude of the people, whereas Matthew says that Jesus did not heal because in this case he *chose* not to heal. He saw their attitude and did not like it, so he did not heal—a significant departure from the earlier text.

In a case like this, scholars generally conclude that Matthew has changed Mark's version to fit his own ideas, to present a particular characterization of Jesus. He does not want to portray a Jesus who is prevented from healing by the attitudes of others, because such a portrayal would imply that Jesus was not all-powerful. In this way Matthew's concept of Jesus influences his telling of the story. We can certainly appreciate why. His enthusiasm for the risen Christ would move him to picture Jesus as magnificently as he could. We see this dynamic constantly in our own heroes, past and present—from George Washington and Davy Crockett to certain modern football coaches. It is one thing to look at the events of Jesus' life, declare him to be the Son of God, and believe in him as such. It is quite another thing to record the events of his life to fit one's own idea of what the Son of God might be like. While Matthew's enthusiasm of faith might be contagious, his alteration of the text obscures a genuine understanding of the events in the life of Jesus. When it concerns such aspects of his life as healing, which his followers are asked to carry on, it proves detrimental to the actual intentions of Jesus.

Scholars have noted a general tendency of the early church to do just this.[5] The healer who proclaims the kingdom of God becomes the proclaimed himself. The work of his life falls into the background of the general proclamation of who he was. The experience and proclamation of the risen Christ color the record of the earthly Jesus. In this way a form of docetism[6] develops within the gospel records. The humanity of Jesus is sacrificed in order to convince the gospel readers of his divinity. To be sure, the early councils of the church did try to preserve a balanced idea of Christ as both fully human and fully divine. However, most of the early church proclamations, including the gospels of Matthew, Luke and John, were strongly influenced by the gnosticism of the day[7]—a theological view according to which the body and physical reality were devalued in favor of the spirit, so that the portrait of Jesus that emerged in the gospels hides some of his human qualities. While the loss of these qualities allowed one to proclaim the divine side more strongly, it also removed qualities from the human side that are essential for healing.

Luke's version of the same passage gives us another example of the tendency of the later evangelists to alter the portrait of Jesus.

And he came to Nazareth, where he had been brought up; and he went to the synagogue, as his custom was, on the sabbath day. And he stood up to read; and there was given to him the book of the prophet Isaiah. He opened the book and found the place where it was written,

"The Spirit of the Lord is upon me,
because he has anointed me
to preach good news to the poor.
He has sent me to proclaim release to the captives
and recovering of sight to the blind,
to set at liberty those who are oppressed,
to proclaim the acceptable year of the Lord."

And he closed the book, and gave it back to the attendant, and sat down; and the eyes of all in the synagogue were fixed on him. And he began to say to them, "Today this scripture has been fulfilled in your hearing." And all spoke well of him, and won-dered at the gracious words which proceeded out of his mouth; and they said, "Is not this Joseph's son?" And he said to them, "Doubtless you will quote to me this proverb, 'Physician, heal yourself; what we have heard you did at Capernaum, do here also in your own country.'" And he said, "Truly, I say to you, no prophet is acceptable in his own country. But in truth, I tell you, there were many widows in Israel in the days of Elijah, when the heaven was shut up three years and six months, when there came a great famine over all the land; and Elijah was sent to none of them but only to Zarephath, in the land of Sidon, to a woman who was a widow. And there were many lepers in Israel in the time of the prophet Elisha; and none of them was cleansed, but only Naaman the Syrian." When they heard this, all in the synagogue were filled with wrath. And they rose up and put him out of the city, and led him to the brow of the hill on which their city was built, that they mighty throw him down headlong. But passing through the midst of them he went away (Lk 4:16–30).

Luke creates a more elaborate story than either Mark or Matthew. Only he introduces the notion that the people sought to kill Jesus. At first the people speak well of him, asking only one question about his family ties: "Is not this Joseph's son?" Luke adds Jesus' quoting of Isaiah, and his announcement of the fulfillment of this prophecy. The Old Testament parallels to Elijah and Elisha are Luke's way of explaining why Jesus did so little healing in his home town. Luke does not want to state that Jesus could not or did not heal. Rather, he offers the Old Testament references as an explanation of why God seems to act in some cases and not in others. He leaves out the issue of the townspeople's attitude as described in Mark, as well as that in Matthew of Jesus choosing not to heal. In Luke the people turn on Jesus after he makes uncomplimentary parallels between them and Old Testament situations. Though more elaborate then Mark's or Matthew's, Luke's approach departs furthest from the original given by Mark.

Another passage from Mark helps to show how differently the evangelists approach the healing stories:

And they came to Bethsaida. And some people brought to him a blind man, and begged him to touch him. And he took the blind man by the hand, led him out of the village; and when he had spit on his eyes and laid his hands upon him, he asked him, "Do you see anything?" And he looked up and said, "I see men; but they look like trees, walking." Then again he laid his hands upon his eyes; and he looked intently and was restored, and saw everything clearly. And he sent him away to his home, saying, "Do not even enter the village" (Mk 8:22–26).

There are many important elements of healing in this story, as we shall see later. First we should note that Matthew and Luke both omit it from their gospels—a curious thing, because this is the only healing story in which Jesus makes two efforts to heal a person. As with the return of Jesus to his home town, Matthew and Luke omit this story of the healing of the blind man because it does not fit into their idea of the type of healer Jesus must have been. Yet the story in Mark not only concerns Jesus, it concerns the man he is healing as well. Similarly, the story of Jesus in his home town told us not just about Jesus but about the townspeople. Healing is as much a product of the person being healed as of the healer. The attitude of those being healed is as important as the attitude of the healer. Some of this lesson is lost in the gospels of Matthew and Luke.

Matthew and Luke probably also omit this story from their gospels because they could not appreciate or accept Jesus' use of spittle in the healing, and its shamanistic style. In another story from Mark, the story of the healing of a deaf man with a speech impediment, Jesus uses spittle to help loosen the man's tongue (Mk 7:31–37). Because this was another aspect of the healings of Jesus they did not like, Matthew and Luke conveniently excluded it also.

Matthew and Luke often embellish the stories they do copy from the gospel of Mark. Each has his own style. In three of the stories he copies from Mark, Matthew has two people healed rather than the one mentioned in Mark.[8] Matthew does not tell any healing story that is not also found in one of the other three gospels. He does however, include general references to healing by Jesus not included in the other three gospels.[9] This is his way of showing his special interest in the healing ministry of Jesus.

Luke goes much further than Matthew in elaborating the tradition of the healings. Tradition holds that Luke was a physician. As such he would be vitally interested in healing. His special interest is demonstrated in his gospel by the inclusion of five healing stories not found in any of the other three gospels. They have different levels of authenticity. One, the healing of the ten lepers, extends the multiple-healing dynamic first seen in Matthew. While this aspect of the story may not be authentic, the story does include elements that probably are (Lk 17:11–19).[10] Others, the healing of the woman with the spirit of infirmity and the healing of the man with dropsy, present authentic healing tradition, but mixed with teaching material important to Luke (Lk 13:10–17; 14:1–6).[11] In yet another, the healing of the widow's son at Nain, Luke tells the story primarily to make Old Testament links, as he did in his version of the story of Jesus returning to his home town (Lk 7:11–17).[12] Finally, Luke adds the story of the healing of the servant's ear in Gethsemane at the time of the betrayal by Judas (Lk 22:47–53). While all the evangelists mention that the servant's ear was cut off, only Luke claims that Jesus healed it. It is hard to imagine why the other evangelists would omit this healing if it actually occurred. Thus it is most likely an addition of Luke to emphasize the healing power of Jesus. We can appreciate why Luke would do this, but we can also see that it distorts the record of just what Jesus did and did not heal. Interestingly, the restoring of a severed ear is not in the province of shamanistic healing. Only the sophisticated technology of modern medicine might restore such a severed member.

As we explore the gospel healing stories in the chapters ahead, we will give preference to those stories that most authentically present the healing work of Jesus. Since Matthew and Luke tend to portray the stories they copied from Mark more in the light of their own thoughts about what kind of healer Jesus must have been, we will use the original version in Mark whenever there are duplicated stories. We will also explore the additional healing stories found in Luke and John.

While there are differences in the way the evangelists present Jesus as a healer, they generally agree on the type of illnesses Jesus healed. (The one major exception is the story in Luke of the severed ear.) These illnesses are mentioned in the particular healing stories and in the general references to the healings of Jesus scattered throughout the gospels.[13] Much of the healing of Jesus has to do with the senses: he healed the blind, the deaf, the dumb, and those with leprosy. As we look at each of these diseases, we will see that they contain elements that make them psychogenic in nature—even in the case of congenital blindness.[14]

Jesus healed paralytics, a man with a withered hand, and people with a crippled condition. The healing that occurs indicates that these conditions were primarily psychogenic and not organic, as in the case of the severed ear. Another group of healings includes the woman with a flow of blood, some fevers, and a man with dropsy. These conditions are generally symptoms of illness, all of them within the range of the work of shamans.

A final category of healing includes epilepsy, demon possession, and the raising of the dead. Demon possession overlaps with some of the other conditions. For example, Jesus heals a deaf and dumb boy by casting out a demon. These conditions, as we shall see, can best be interpreted from a shamanistic and psychological viewpoint. Because of their unique nature for the western mind, we shall devote a chapter each to the casting out of demons and the raising of the dead. We continue by exploring first the casting out of demons.

NOTES

[1] The reader is referred to books that present the gospels in parallel columns, making it easy to see where they are similar and where they are different. *Gospel Parallels,* edited by Burton H. Throckmorton, Jr., presents

the Revised Standard Version of the three synoptic gospels in parallel columns. *Synopsis of the Four Gospels,* edited by Kurt Aland, presents parallel columns of all four gospels in both Greek and English.

[2] All biblical quotes are from *The New Oxford Annotated Bible* (Revised Standard Version).

[3] Jerome Frank, M.D., "The Medical Power of Faith."

[4] Research using a placebo involves one group that takes a prescribed medicine and another group that takes a harmless milk sugar pill. Both groups are told what the pill is expected to do. Often in such studies both groups will show the expected results. In the case of those taking the placebo the results come solely because of the expectations of those taking the pill. Chapter 2 of Norman Cousins' *The Anatomy of an Illness* offers a good discussion of the placebo.

[5] See Günther Bornkamn, *Jesus of Nazareth,* Chapter 9. We will pick up this theme again in Chapter 12.

[6] Docetism is a tendency in Christian thought, dating back to the first century, to diminish the humanity of Jesus.

[7] Gnostic sects within Christianity usually devalued the physical and material aspects of life.

[8] Two demoniacs appear in Matthew 8:28–34 compared to one in Mark 5:1–20, two blind men appear in Matthew 9:27–31 compared to the one in Mark 10:46–52, and two blind men appear in Matthew 20:29–30 compared to the one in Mark 10:46–52.

[9] Mt 4:23–24; 9:35; 15:29–31; 19:1–2; and 21:14 are general references to healing by Jesus found only in Matthew's gospel.

[10] Discussed in detail in Chapter 9.

[11] Discussed in detail in Chapter 5.

[12] Discussed in detail in Chapter 11.

[13] General references to the healings of Jesus in the gospels include Mk 1:32–34 (parallels in Mt 8:16 and Lk 4:40), Mk 3:10 (parallels in Mt 12:15 and Lk 6:18–19), Mk 6:56 (parallel in Mt 14:36), Mt 11:4–5 (parallel in Lk 7:21–22), Mt 14:14 (parallel in Lk 9:11); Lk 5:15, 8:2, and 13:32; Jn 6:2 and 7:23. References found only in Matthew are listed in note 9.

[14] See R.K. Harrison's article, "Disease," in *The Interpreter's Dictionary of the Bible,* especially the section "Disease of the NT." His section under "Healing," entitled "The Approach of Jesus to Health and Healing," is a good overview of the healing work of Jesus.

Chapter 3
Casting Out Demons

As we try to understand the gospel stories in which Jesus casts out demons, it is helpful to remember the resemblance between Jesus and healing shamans. To Jesus, illness is often the work of demons. The healing process unfolds when a particular demon, or sometimes more than one, is driven out of a person. This may be perplexing to modern ears, but it is unfair to the gospel record and to other healing traditions to merely write it off as primitive thinking. Depth psychology in particular helps us see that early people did not have an inferior way of evaluating human nature, health, and illness. Rather, western culture has lost its ability to see a spiritual world consisting of both helpful and not-so-helpful spirits and demons.

Let us put it another way. Today children are closer to inner reality than most adults. When the sun goes down and darkness sets in, the world of demons and monsters comes alive for children. They peer from outside windows, they hide in the closets, under the bed, up in the attic, and down in the cellar. During the day these places contain the usual paraphernalia as any adult will gladly point out. Yet conversations with many adults indicate that when night falls even they experience fears and imaginative wanderings that normally do not arise during the day.

We can distinguish between daytime thinking and nighttime thinking. Ours is primarily a daytime-thinking culture. We like to see life as we know it when the sun is shining and the world can be seen objectively. If we or our children run across the inhabitants of the night, we like to say it is "only" our imagination. We turn on a light to show our children (and ourselves) that there are only shoes and clothes in the closet, nothing else. We rely on daytime thinking. When it fails us, which is often the case, we lock our outside doors, clothes closets, attics, and cellars, and keep our feet from touching the floor around the bed until dawn the next day. It is in the daylight world that we excel, that we are productive and at home.

We are not at home in the nighttime world. Our attempts to contact the world of spirits compare feebly to those of shamans and religious figures of earlier cultures. Their myths and rituals describe nighttime reality at length. They are so at home in this world that they have even named its inhabitants. The figures of ancient Greek mythology and the Kachinas of the Zuni Pueblo Indians of New Mexico and Arizona are good examples; helpful spirits aid healing and enhance human life, while unclean spirits bring illness and restrict life. Our "night life" is inferior, and as long as we tell ourselves and our children that our demons are not really there, or that they are "only in our imaginations," it will remain so.

The idea of an inner world is very helpful in this regard. For in night-time thinking it is this inner world that we experience. The characters that come from within us at night have their own life and their own stories. If we know their stories as depicted in myth and ritual, we are better able to know where our own lives are unfolding, and whether it is in a healing direction. The creative imagination can help enormously in bringing these inner realities into focus. We can become much more conscious of our inner dynamics and of how God might be moving within us.

The psychology of C.G. Jung goes a long way in explaining our night-time world. In his life, as well as his psychological work, Jung spoke of how important it is to find the images behind our feelings and emotions.[1] In these images Jung perceived common patterns and motifs that he called archetypal patterns. They are found not only in the inner life of modern people, but in ancient myths and rituals. The characters are gods, spirits, and demons of earlier times. More ancient people, including Jesus, believed it possible for individuals to be possessed by demons. The goal of the healer was to free the person from such influence and put him in touch with the spirit of healing.

In Jung's psychology, a person comes under the influence of a particular complex that prevents the full unfolding of the personality. A man or woman may suffer from a mother complex, for example. Such a person lives by the values of his mother, and his feeling life resides in her psychology. He becomes ill, physically or psychologically, when this influence becomes so strong that other parts of the personality suffer. For healing to take place, the mother complex must be integrated, a process in which the psychotherapist can help. When at length a balance begins to come forth, the strain on the body is lessened.

Discernment in this inner world comes only with experience. Often inner figures that seem threatening at first are bringing healing, while those that seem good can be opposed both to healing and to God.

An example is the angel Lucifer, or "lightbearer," who thought he could do a better job than God. Someone can be said to be possessed by Lucifer when, in the name of light, he claims to know the divine order of things in the face of solid evidence to the contrary. This demon plays on our human tendency to want to have life our own way. The stronger it becomes, the less likely it is that a person will hear God's voice. Similarly, such a demon preys on the part of a person that likes to be cared for, stroked, and to be the center of attention. Very likely, such a person would carry on an "if" relationship with God—something like, "If things go my way and life is comfortable for me, I will believe in you." Ironically, such a person invites discomfort and even illness: as we shall see, this is often the only way God can get our attention and help us see that we might have a demon.

Jung's work bridges shamanism and western thought by taking shamanism seriously and demonstrating that a relationship to the vast inner world—the collective unconscious, in his phrase—is crucial to one's health. Jung describes this inner world and its archetypal patterns in clear, modern language. For him experience is the key to understanding the inner life. He invites those in search of healing, or of God, to encounter this world through their personal experience.

Jesus was at home in the realm of demons, in nighttime reality. It was natural for him to talk about them in the course of his healing work. This is one reason why he taught that unless we are like little children, we cannot enter the kingdom of heaven (Mt 18:1–5). Children are close to the nighttime world; unless adults can maintain this same relationship, they will lose touch with the inner kingdom of heaven.

One reason Jesus was so at home in the night world had to do with the Judaism of his day. In the Jewish cycle of life, each day began at sunset, the time of darkness, and ended with the time of daylight. One lived first in night life and then in day life. The creation story in the book of Genesis begins in darkness. From darkness comes light. The Jewish calendar and all its feast days were based on the moon and determined by its cycles. Generally the moon can only be seen at night. Thus the ancient Hebrews, like most primitive peoples, were especially adept at looking into life at night.

From very early in its history, Christianity adopted the Roman calendar and began to base its year on the sun rather than the moon. The old lunar calendar was traded in for a solar one. This change symbolized the transition in consciousness that has permeated western culture. Modern science has benefited, but the type of healing ministry found in the gospels has suffered greatly. At times the Christian mystical tradition has pointed back toward the inner world and the mysterious ways of darkness: John of the Cross is noted for his sixteenth century work *The Dark Night of the Soul.*[2] But such mystics are the exception.

Most modern Christians practice their religion along the lines of day-time consciousness. Whereas the Jews held their family meals and religious services beginning with dusk and the coming of night, most of today's Christian services are daytime events. Those in the evening are held then for the practical reason of attendance rather than for any spiritual purpose. There are two exceptions. One is the Christmas Eve service, which, for a number of denominations, is the principal service of Christmas. Here is a great Christian service centered in the time of darkness. Its timing, though, is rooted in the ancient *non*-Christian winter solstice ceremonies rather than in early Christian practice. Still, it affords Christians an opportunity to come into some general contact with the spiritual mysteries of darkness and the night.

More recently here in the west there has been a movement to restore the great vigil of Easter on Easter eve. This does not call forth the popular response of Christmas, but there does appear to be growing interest in many churches. In very early Christianity the Easter vigil was the central service of the year. Following Jewish practice, it actually began with the setting of the sun on Saturday, lasting through the night until dawn the next day. For the early church the full mystery of Easter, the central event of Christian belief, was experienced as the time of darkness finally moved into the time of light. During this great service all baptisms were performed, and those baptized received the eucharist for the first time. The resurrection took place at night! At dawn the tomb was empty; Jesus was already risen.

This celebration of the great vigil of Easter continues in eastern Christianity. Westerners often have trouble becoming accustomed to an Easter service at night; many who attend a vigil service feel they have not been to church on Easter and return the following day for a daytime service. Certainly this inclination is largely due to custom. However, it is also due to our having become almost exclusively a daytime culture, out of touch with the side of spiritual reality that lies within nature's cycle of darkness. Consequently we lack access to an important area of spiritual wisdom.

Nighttime thinking allows us to approach the world of demons. In his healing, Jesus used the same approach, and we turn next to examine his healing work more closely.

The Healing of the Demonic in the Synagogue

Mark sets the stage for Jesus' ministry of casting out demons with this story:

And immediately there was in their synagogue a man with an unclean spirit; and he cried out, "What have you to do with us, Jesus of Nazareth? Have you come to destroy us? I know who you are, the Holy One of God." But Jesus rebuked him, saying, "Be silent, and come out of him!" And the unclean spirit, convulsing him and crying with a loud voice, came out of him. And they were all amazed, so that they questioned among themselves, saying, "What is this? A new teaching! With authority he commands even the unclean spirits, and they obey him" (Mk 1:23–27).

In this story Mark indicates that Jesus casts out demons. More importantly, he indicates that Jesus' very presence makes the existence of the unclean spirit clear. We recognize the man as having an unclean spirit when it begins to speak out because of the presence of Jesus. Mark tells us that before meeting this man Jesus had entered the synagogue on the sabbath and taught—not as the scribes, but as one who had authority. Jesus brought a much higher level of spiritual and psychological awareness into the synagogue, one that revealed the existence of previously unrecognized demons. This is a crucial aspect of Jesus' healing ministry: he heals because he has a much deeper spiritual and psychological consciousness than contemporary religious leaders. He sees far more deeply into nighttime reality.

There is a good parallel in psychotherapy. Some people come to therapy not because of any specific problem, but because they do not feel quite right within themselves. Others come for some external reason, but in both cases an exploration of their internal life reveals that they are at least somewhat "possessed by a demon." Certain attitudes or values have subtly come to paralyze their life and cut off the flow of a more creative spirit. Psychotherapeutic work can be seen as bringing to awareness the "unclean spirit," so that the more creative life energy can come forth. Often, though, the new life feels threatening and is mistaken for the unclean spirit. For example, a woman dreamed that Satan was playing loud radio music from unexplored rooms of her childhood home. After exploring the source of the sound from room to room, she tried to get this demon to leave. Further exploration revealed that the rooms were taboo because her mother had felt that what they represented was of the devil. As it turned out, through the radio music the spirit was trying to turn her attention to areas of her life and personality that she had neglected. The real demon was the voice of her mother, devaluing these aspects of life. What she heard over the radio was the healing voice of God.

This gospel story presents a similar paradox. Imagine finding an unclean spirit in a synagogue on the sabbath! Yet when Jesus enters, one is revealed. The spiritual awareness of those in the synagogue is too low to recognize that the unclean spirit is in the man. But, faced with the presence of Jesus, the spirit knows that it is in trouble. Again we can see parallels to psychotherapy. Meeting with a therapist or spiritual guide who has the necessary degree of consciousness to assist him, a person's unclean spirit will be recognized. This is not an easy task in most cases, because the unclean spirit prefers to hide. Exposure is crucial, however, if the person is going to go forward in health.

The discovery of the unclean spirit in this story raises important questions. It is the spirit that raises them! "What have you to do with us, Jesus of Nazareth? Have you come to destroy us?" The answer will unfold throughout the gospels. No, Jesus will not destroy them. They might always return. But he will cast them out and silence them so that the true voice of God will be heard. Mark tells us, "But Jesus rebuked him, saying, 'Be silent, and come out of him!' " Many psychotherapeutic patients have a negative voice within them, telling them they are no good and will never amount to much. The work of therapy assists in neutralizing such voices so that the voice of God within can emerge and lead the person to a more fulfilled and God-centered life.

For the voice of God to be heard, it was necessary that the unclean spirit be driven out. Such things never go easily, and Mark tells us that as it came out the "unclean spirit" convulsed the man and cried out in a loud voice. Likewise, in psychotherapy, casting out the negative voice or old life patterns is often difficult and painful. There is a crying out and a convulsing of sorts before a more healing path can be taken. The new way is threatening because it means casting out the old, with which the person has been closely identified. As this work progresses, new energy and excitement for life emerges. Finally there is celebration of the new way, and a sense of power over the unclean spirit.

The unclean spirit in this story raises one final question. Those in the temple ask, "What is this? A new teaching!" The ability of Jesus to cast out demons and bring healing suggests a new wisdom. Using not just words, like those usually heard in the synagogue, this wisdom expresses itself through healing.

The Gerasene Demoniac

The next incident of the casting out of a demon in Mark is the story of the Gerasene demoniac.

They came to the other side of the sea, to the country of the Gerasenes. And when he had come out of the boat, there met him out of the tombs a man with an unclean spirit, who lived among the tombs; and no one could bind him any more, even with a chain; for he had often been bound with fetters and chains, but the chains he wrenched apart, and the fetters he broke in pieces; and no one had the strength to subdue him. Night and day among the tombs and on the mountains he was always crying out, and bruising himself with stones. And when he saw Jesus from afar, he ran and worshipped him; and crying out with a loud voice, he said, "What have you to do with me, Jesus, Son of the Most High God? I adjure you by God, do not torment me." For he had said to him, "Come out of the man, you unclean spirit!" And Jesus asked him, "What is your name?" He replied, "My name is Legion; for we are many." And he begged him eagerly not to send them out of the country. Now a great herd of swine was feeding there on the hillside; and they begged him, "Send us to the swine, let us enter them." So he gave them leave. And the unclean spirits came out, and entered the swine; and the herd, numbering about two thousand, rushed down the steep bank into the sea, and were drowned in the sea.
   The herdsmen fled, and told it in the city and in the country. And people came to see what it was that had happened. And they came to Jesus, and saw the demoniac sitting there, clothed and in his right mind, the man who had had the legion; and they were afraid. And those who had seen it told what had happened to the demoniac and to the swine. And they began to beg Jesus to depart from their neighborhood. And as he was getting into the boat, the man who had been possessed with demons begged him that he might be with him. But he refused, and said to him, "Go home to your friends, and tell them how much the Lord has done for you, and how he has had mercy on you." And he went away

and began to proclaim in the Decapolis how much Jesus had done for him; and all men marveled (Mk 5:1–20).

This story is full of many subtle and important details. When Jesus comes out of the boat, the man with the unclean spirit comes out of the tombs where he lived. A graveyard is a strange place to live, but it tells us something psychologically. Graveyards and cemeteries are places for nighttime spirits. Children in particular often sense the inner imaginative world when they are in such places, especially when it is dark. The imagination runs freely here, immersing us in nighttime reality, in what Jung called the collective unconscious.[3] The man's living in the tombs suggests that he had become overwhelmed by the unconscious and probably suffered from some form of psychosis. That "no one could bind him" and "no one had the strength to subdue him" supports this hypothesis. Occasionally such a person exhibits tremendous strength and energy and is hard to control. It is as if the ego, which usually channels a person's energies, has been dissipated, can no longer control his inner energies, and cannot restrain his great strength. We also hear that the demoniac was bruising himself with stones. Like some psychotics, he had no sense of pain, no sense of being separate from the demon that possessed him; he did not know that he was injuring himself.

Considering the extent of this man's turmoil, we see an amazing change as soon as he becomes aware of Jesus. The change begins even as he sees Jesus from afar, as if the tumultuous spirits within him recognized an even greater spirit. While physical intervention with this man proves fruitless, the proper spiritual presence begins to change him dramatically. The man runs and worships Jesus. At the same time he asks a question similar to the one we heard in the previous story: "What have you to do with me, Jesus, Son of the Most High God? I adjure you by God, do not torment me." He fears the anticipated transformation. Will the demon be destroyed? Will the man be destroyed as the two forces, the unclean spirit and the spirit within Jesus, encounter one another? As in the previous story, neither happens. The unclean spirit is not destroyed; but it must step aside for the greater healing spirit to enter. Neither is the man himself destroyed in the process.

We notice in this healing story and in others involving a demon that Jesus talks with it. Here he asks, "What is your name?" From the psychological perspective this is a crucial question. Naming of something makes it more conscious. The more conscious we are of the dynamics inside us, the more we can cast aside "unclean spirits" so that the Spirit of God can flow through us. The less conscious we are of such things, the more they rule our lives, and the less centered in God we are likely to be.

There is a good example of the significance of naming in the Old Testament story of Jacob. The name Jacob means "deceiver" or "supplanter." In this story Jacob first cons his brother Esau out of his birthright and later deceives his father Isaac into giving him Esau's blessing as the firstborn son. Later, after Jacob has undergone a significant personality change and wrestled with God at the river Jabbok (another nighttime experience), he receives a new name, Israel, which means "he who strives with God" or "he who wrestles with God."[4]

Inner dialogue can be crucial to "naming" our inner demons and making us more conscious of them. One woman in therapy came to discover three such characters in herself, who would often lead her away from her true path and her true personality. She came to terms with these characters by looking at her dreams and doing imaginative work with many of the figures that appeared. Through a process Jung called active imagination, the woman named these three characters and began to lessen their power over her. She gave them the names of three Greek gods. To her surprise, two of the figures often appeared in her dreams as clergymen. They seemed to offer guidance but in reality kept her off a healing path. Coming to terms with these inner figures enabled her to begin lifting a general state of depression that had been with her for over twenty years. During that time she had tried a number of other approaches, including medication, consultation with a clinical psychologist, and the healing of memories technique with a clergyman.

In the case of the Gerasene demoniac, when Jesus asked for the demon's name the answer was, "My name is Legion; for we are many." Not only is it possible for people to have a demon, it is possible to have many. The gospels tell us that Jesus drove seven demons out of Mary Magdalene.[5] That this man's demons cannot be counted may also indicate a psychotic condition. He does not have enough ego base even to count them, let alone name them. The contents of the unconscious have overwhelmed him completely. Yet Jesus provides a centering experience that drives off the demons and gives the man new life.

It is important to note that the idea of demons does not necessarily imply psychosis. Unconscious complexes and archetypes affect us all. Most of us have the ego strength to relate to them. Denying them and letting them remain unconscious allows them more influence over our lives. "Demons" or "unclean spirits" can lie behind anything from depression, to disharmony in relationships, to physical illness. Removing the symptoms does not necessarily imply that we have dealt with the aspect of our inner life that may have created the symptoms to begin with.

At the turn of the century psychosis was very little understood. Before it entered the domain of medical science, psychotic people were assumed to have demons. But because they were seen as being possessed by a demon, they were dismissed, ignored, and tortured. Demon possession meant that one could do nothing for them—just the opposite of Jesus' work in the gospels. Generally, when people use such terminology today it is to refer to something they do not understand or do not like; they are dismissing certain aspects of human life and affliction rather than healing them. In the gospels it is just the opposite.

Although foreign to most modern thinking, the use of words like "demons" and "unclean spirits" finds natural parallels in Jung's psychology.[6] He calls them complexes and demonstrates how they are present in all of us, influencing who we are and what we become. The more consciously we recognize such aspects of ourselves, the more we allow the deepest healing spirit of God to emerge. Unlike Freud, Jung was heavily involved in work with schizophrenics and other psychotic patients. He began his psychiatric career in the Burgholzi Mental Health Hospital in Zurich, where he came to realize that the hidden dynamics in these patients were only extensions of what goes on in each of us. While today Jungians work mostly with neurotics, people whose basic ego structure is still intact, this approach has proved valuable with psychotic patients as well.[7]

To go the way of the Father, Jesus too had to wrestle with the voices within himself. As we have seen, he taught primarily about the kingdom of heaven, a spiritual kingdom that provides insight into our inner nature.[8] The best example of this work in the life of Jesus himself is his wrestling with the devil in the wilderness immediately after his baptism.[9] If he had not handled this encounter successfully, he would not have understood properly the meaning of his baptism or followed his unique call from God. His wilderness experience also helped him when the voice of others might have led him astray. When Jesus first began to tell his disciples what lay ahead, the important dialogue at Caesarea Philippi, Peter could not accept it. When Jesus announced that he must suffer many things from the elders, chief priests, and scribes, and be killed, and on the third day be raised, Peter exclaimed, "God forbid, Lord! This shall never happen to you" (Mt 16:22). Jesus immediately recognized Peter's statement as the voice of Satan. If he had not wrestled with this voice in the wilderness, he might not have recognized it speaking through Peter. These experiences indicated that voices speak in each of us, and we must wrestle with them so that we can know and follow God's call.

In the passage at hand, Jesus helped the Gerasene demoniac do what many of us cannot do alone. He helped him to become more conscious of the nature of the demons within him and to become free of their influence. But as we have seen, the demons must go somewhere; they cannot be destroyed. This forces us to stay alert to the call of God. If we thought they were totally destroyed, we would probably let our guard down and not work at finding and fulfilling God's will. In this case, at their request, Jesus lets these unclean spirits enter a great herd of swine. Swine were a good choice: the Jews considered them ritually unclean and were not allowed to eat them. Having the unclean spirits enter the swine removed them as far from others as possible.[10]

At this point an extraordinary thing happened. When the unclean spirits entered the herd, which numbered about two thousand, they rushed down a steep bank into the sea and were drowned. Scholars point out an interesting fact about this part of the story: the town of Gerasa which Mark mentions as the scene of this incident is actually thirty miles from the sea. Accordingly, later manuscripts or translations substitute the name of a site closer to the sea. There is little doubt by most scholars today that Mark actually wrote "Gerasa." There are two interpretations: either the swine ran a long way before they were drowned, or the mention of the sea is to be taken symbolically. As it happens, water and the sea are usually symbols of the unconscious, the source of all psychological and spiritual life. In this sense the story can be taken to indicate that, cast out by Jesus from this man's life at Gerasa, the unclean spirits were forced back into the spiritual realm or collective unconscious.

This part of the story also gives a good feeling for the tremendous power of the unclean spirits. When we see them drown the herd of swine, the demoniac appears not as one weak and possessed, but as a figure of great strength. If all these swine were destroyed, how did he ever survive? Here another parallel with psychotherapy presents itself. It is amazing how much people will allow themselves to suffer before they seek assistance and begin the process of sorting out the unclean spirits that assault them from within. Part of the reason people put off seeking help is that they do not want to appear weak or face the social stigma of needing help. Thus, paradoxically, people coming to therapy are often not weak but have great inner strength and courage. When someone is finally at his wits' end and seeks help, he may be ready to become conscious of his unclean spirits and respond to his healing center. The so-called maladjusted sufferers of our society often turn out to be creative, caring, sensitive, and courageous.

The next part of the story reflects another area of experience that is common today. When something dramatic takes place, people like to run off and talk about it, like the herdsmen in the story. When others hear about a dramatic event, they often come out to explore what is happening. People have a natural curiosity. In this story, as they realize what is happening, they become afraid. Experience of the inner world, the unconscious, is both attractive and frightening. It is best not denied, yet it cannot be taken lightly. Such experience can be especially frightening when healing is involved. Despite their curiosity, the townspeople who came out to see Jesus and the cured demoniac ask Jesus to leave. His healing capacity is too much of a challenge for them to live with.

Further insights into this story arise from a consideration of the situation of the man involved after the healing. For one thing, we read that he is clothed. This implies that he had been naked or very disheveled—so overwhelmed by the unclean spirits that he did not have a proper relationship with his day-to-day life. Now that he is clothed, his capacity to relate to the everyday side of life has been restored. This change is so remarkable that it frightens those who have come out to see him.

We are also told that this man is now "in his right mind." The "right mind" is synonymous with the functioning of a conscious ego. Previously, this man's ego consciousness was lost because so many figures had emerged from his unconscious.

In most situations the problem is that the functioning of the ego dominates other parts of the personality, excluding them from consciousness. Life is viewed one-sidedly and from an incomplete psychological and spiritual perspective. Jesus offers a spiritual prescription for such a condition:

> If your right eye causes you to sin, pluck it out and throw it away;
> it is better that you lose one of your members than that your
> whole body be thrown into hell. And if your right hand causes
> you to sin, cut it off and throw it away; it is better that you lose
> one of your members than that your whole body go into hell (Mt
> 5:29–30).

The right eye and right hand represent what is most in our conscious
control. Psychologically, we must often sacrifice this in order to find our
whole being. The man from Gerasa had a more unusual problem: he
needed to have his ego capacity restored. For though ego consciousness
can lead to spiritual one-sidedness, without it we cannot make the choices
and decisions necessary to respond to God's call.

At the conclusion of the story it is time for Jesus to leave, as the people
from the surrounding countryside have begged him to do. When Jesus
prepares to go, the man who had been possessed begs to go with him. But
Jesus refuses. He sees that it is best for the man not to follow him, but to
stay where he is. Jesus invites others to follow him after he has healed
them, but not this man. Now that the unclean spirits have been driven
away, the man must get back into life on his own. It is important for him to
use his restored ego consciousness and no longer rely on Jesus. With a
restored ego and the remembrance of how Jesus confronted the demons
within him, he has the tools necessary to confront them again, should they
ever return. This is the purpose of much therapy—to strengthen the ego
and help the person come to grips with "unclean demons" until he can
deal with them himself. This, it seems, is all that God calls some people
to do.

Jesus asks this man to go to his friends and "tell them how much the
Lord has done for you, and how he has had mercy on you." His instructions are tailored to this particular individual. In his teaching and encounters with others Jesus says the opposite. For example, in Matthew
10:35–36 we hear him say, "For I have come to set a man against his
father, and a daughter against her mother, and a daughter-in-law against
her mother-in-law; and a man's foes will be those of his own household."
Jesus challenges most people to leave home and live their lives in the world,
following God's call. But he sends this particular man home. Jesus simply
wants him to talk about his experience, to share with others what has

happened to him. This can be compared to the work of people in Alcoholics Anonymous. While AA has no denominational affiliation, its work has a spiritual base. AA has the best record of all groups in healing alcoholism. A large part of the program is the sharing of experience. Members share with each other and with new people their struggles with the "demon" of alcoholism and how they were able to begin their day-to-day sobriety. The demoniac's healing can be seen in this light. It came through no action of his own. He made no personal journey for healing. It was by the grace of God that Jesus happened on the scene. In this case, it is enough for this man to go and tell others of the healing that has come to him.

Not until the final verse of the story are we assured that the healing is complete. We have seen that it entailed the driving out of many unclean spirits and the restoration of ego consciousness. Because this was an experience of grace, his ego consciousness can be seen as a gift from God. If he had not used this gift as God intended—for example, tried to follow Jesus despite his instructions—he might have been possessed again.[11] But the man does exactly as he is asked, putting his gift to work proclaiming how much Jesus has done for him. He has accepted God's call to him and acts it out despite any anxieties or fears. The appropriateness of this action for him is borne out in the last words of the story when we hear that "all men marveled." Because of the healing and his acceptance of Jesus' instructions, good fruit now comes forth from his life.

The Syrophoenician Woman

Mark's narrative of the Syrophoenician woman is his next account of the casting out of a demon. This time the demon is in a child, and a request for healing is made by the mother on her behalf.

> And from there he arose and went away to the region of Tyre and Sidon. And he entered a house, and would not have any one know it; yet he could not be hid. But immediately a woman, whose little daughter was possessed by an unclean spirit, heard of him, and came and fell down at his feet. Now the woman was a Greek, a Syrophoenician by birth. And she begged him to cast the demon out of her daughter. And he said to her, "Let the children first be fed, for it is not right to take the children's bread and throw it to the dogs." But she answered him, "Yes, Lord; yet even the dogs under the table eat the children's crumbs." And he said to her, "For this saying you may go your way; the demon

has left your daughter." And she went home, and found the child
lying in bed, and the demon gone (Mk 7:24–30).

Our primary interest here is the release of the daughter through the
efforts of the mother. Jesus' final remark indicates that an important transformation has taken place in the mother.[12] When this transformation happens, the daughter is freed of her demon.

Psychotherapy shows that there is nothing simple about a child having a problem. The difficulty often reflects the family situation.[13] The
child's problem may not be the real issue, but a symptom of it. In this story,
the real problem—and the potential for healing—lies with the mother. She
has not been living her full personality. The daughter's condition stirs her
to action. Though she does not begin by seeking healing for herself, her
search comes from deep within. Her instincts tell her that if she is to find
healing for her daughter, she should seek the help of this Jewish teacher
and healer, even though culturally it would not be appropriate for her, as a
Syrophoenician woman, to approach him.

When she finds Jesus he puts her off for these very reasons. As a Jew,
he believes he is called to assist only the children of Israel. He will not assist
a non-Israelite "dog." But the woman will not let herself be put off. She
pursues her instinct to go to him for help, not allowing this great religious
teacher to keep her from speaking out. Jesus immediately recognizes her
determination, a most important personality trait for healing. She implies,
using Jesus' own imagery, that as far as healing goes, there should always
be enough to go around. Jesus changes his mind about this woman. As she
now speaks from the full depth of her personality, he indicates to her that
her daughter is healed and the demon gone.

In any family or group, when one person begins to change and seeks
to grow, it can affect the whole group. For example, a family brings in an
adolescent boy for counseling. He is beginning to have problems in school
and rebel more at home. When the parents are out of the house he has
friends over and they raid the father's liquor cabinet. The youth has no
idea why he does these things; he just does them. He recognizes that he
does not like the atmosphere at home. He has particular difficulty relating
to his mother. Since his parents see him as the problem, the counseling
entails helping him make the inevitable break from his parents and learn to
go out and live on his own in a responsible way.

Interviews with the parents reveal some interesting facts. The father,
a traveling salesman, has been involved in an affair with another woman.

No one in the family knows about this, but as is often the case, it influences the general family atmosphere. The family is possessed by a demon, so to speak, that hinders proper relationship. Its symptoms appear in the life of the son and of the father as well. However, the mother cannot be exonerated, for she too contributes to the family's unhealthy emotional patterns. She has become very much of a nag to her husband and son. They in response find it very difficult to relate to her. She unconsciously makes the wound deeper rather than healing it. The open revelation of the whole family situation helps ease the tension at home. Life becomes easier for the son because his parents no longer use him as a scapegoat for their problems. Both parents realize that they have work to do on their marriage, as well as on other family relationships. In this way the demon that had originally caused the problems is wrestled with and cast out. Many other people hide behind their children—often just one child, the so-called black sheep—as scapegoats in order to avoid their own responsibility for growth and development.

Unfortunately, this is not an isolated situation. Our society does not provide many avenues for growth in the areas of feeling and personal relationships. We educate only a part of the personality. Men who work in technical and impersonal situations find it difficult to come home and switch to the feeling level of interaction required in families. They become separated from their feelings and what Jung called the anima, the feminine side of their personality. Because they cut themselves off from it, they become subject to moods and emotional outbursts that are outside of their control, a form of mini-possession.[14] Men so possessed often blame their wives and at the same time expect them to fix whatever is wrong. But the problem is not really with the wives; it is with the men themselves. Some men, like our salesman, will have an affair, which is very often only a vain attempt to find their lost creative side. This in turn alienates them further from a genuine feeling relationship with their wives and children, normally the best place to develop these neglected sides of the personality.

A woman, on the other hand, might think it is her fault that her family relationships do not go well. As a result, she becomes harder on herself, wondering what she is doing wrong and trying to correct what cannot be corrected—because the problem is within. A woman who takes this attitude likewise loses touch with her own true feelings and becomes a shell of her real self. She always tries to "adjust" to her husband completely. If only she could do a better job of pleasing him, she feels.

Other women are pulled in the opposite direction, like the woman in our example. They look for a scapegoat, a child or husband, whom they try to change for the better. They nag and berate (for the person's own good, of course) and cease to relate openly and honestly to those around them. They worry primarily about how the family will look to others, rather than about the genuine quality of family life and the individuals in it.

Women in such situations come under the negative influence of what Jung called the animus, the masculine aspect of their personality. It speaks to them as a voice or voices within that berate their true personality and keep them from being themselves. Such a voice or voices might also push a woman to base her life on ideals or conventions that do not square with her deeper values. Usually this negative voice is speaking when she pushes others in a similar way. The positive side of the animus, however, allows a woman to express, and have the courage to live from, her true personality.[15]

As she searches for healing for her daughter, the woman in our gospel story discovers healing for herself as well. She goes to Jesus motivated by genuine love and concern for her daughter, not out of embarrassment at her daughter's condition. Her daughter's illness helps her to connect to her own deep feelings and to follow wherever they might lead. When she does not waver during her encounter with Jesus, it is clear she has reached an important point in her own growth and development.

Before leaving this story I would like to mention the book (and movie) *The Exorcist* and the mother-daughter relationship at its heart.[16] Again, it is the daughter who becomes the victim of the possession, while the underlying spiritual problem that allows it to emerge lies with the mother.[17] The mother has lived exclusively for her career. She is not aware of the unfinished psychological business from the relationship with her estranged husband, to whom she refers early on as a demon—a good indication that there is a demon in *her*. The demonic situation is resolved through the intervention of two priests, who both lose their lives in the process. While they bring about the young girl's dramatic recovery, the mother's underlying problem is not dealt with. The more consciously we live our unresolved conflicts, the more likely it is that down the road someone will pay a heavy price.

The gospel story of the Syrophoenician woman is of great importance. The profound transformation of a mother brings healing to her daughter. The woman is a beautiful paradigm for healing in our time: as we heal ourselves, we will heal others. The story demonstrates that the healing of Jesus worked at a deeper level than that depicted in *The Exorcist*.

Jesus does not forfeit his life in the process but continues to live fully, like
the Syrophoenician woman. In Chapter 9 we will return to her transformation and the impact she had on Jesus because of it.

The Boy Possessed by a Spirit

The final major account in Mark of Jesus casting out a demon or
unclean spirit involves a father and son.

> And when they came to the disciples, they saw a great crowd
> about them, and scribes arguing with them. And immediately all
> the crowd, when they saw him, were greatly amazed, and ran up
> to him and greeted him. And he asked them, "What are you
> discussing with them?" And one of the crowd answered him,
> "Teacher, I brought my son to you, for he has a dumb spirit; and
> wherever it seizes him, it dashes him down; and he foams and
> grinds his teeth and becomes rigid; and I asked your disciples to
> cast it out, and they were not able." And he answered them, "O
> faithless generation, how long am I to be with you? How long am
> I to bear with you? Bring him to me." And they brought the boy
> to him; and when the spirit saw him, immediately it convulsed
> the boy, and he fell on the ground and rolled about, foaming at
> the mouth. And Jesus asked this father, "How long has he had
> this?" And he said, "From childhood. And it has often cast him
> into the fire and into the water, to destroy him; but if you can do
> anything, have pity on us and help us." And Jesus said to him, "If
> you can! All things are possible to him who believes." Immedi-
> ately the father of the child cried out and said, "I believe; help
> my unbelief!" And when Jesus saw that a crowd came running
> together, he rebuked the unclean spirit, saying to it, "You dumb
> and deaf spirit, I command you, come out of him, and never
> enter him again." And after crying out and convulsing him terri-
> bly, it came out, and the boy was like a corpse; so that most of
> them said, "He is dead." But Jesus took him by the hand and
> lifted him up, and he arose. And when he had entered the house,
> his disciples asked him privately, "Why could we not cast it out?"
> And he said to them, "This kind cannot be driven out by any-
> thing but prayer" (Mk 9:14–29).

As if to balance the story about the healing of a daughter through the
mother's transformation, we now hear a story about the healing of a

father's son. Here it is the father who brings the boy for healing. As the father is transformed and becomes more spiritually centered, the son is healed. This father, like the Syrophoenician woman, is deeply concerned about his child and willing to go as far as necessary for healing. Because the boy is possessed by a dumb spirit and cannot talk, Jesus must speak with the father. He cannot engage the spirit directly, as he did with the Gerasene demoniac. Again we find a parallel to modern psychotherapy, where a child's problem is resolved by the direct involvement of parents in the healing process.

As this story opens, Jesus is returning from the transfiguration experience with Peter, James, and John. The other disciples are arguing with the scribes, and a great crowd has gathered. Jesus asks his disciples what they are discussing. Before they can answer, the boy's father speaks up, saying that he brought his son to Jesus because of a demon; he asked the disciples to cast it out, but they were not able. The man is desperate. He and Jesus are soon in dialogue. The disciples are now quiet. Jesus gives an admonition about the "faithless generation," implying that his own disciples have much to learn. After expressing his frustration, Jesus immediately seeks to understand the boy's difficulties. The father is also anxious for healing, but for a different reason. He is in agony over his son's situation. His son's condition presses him to find healing and to make things happen. He is strongly motivated to seek healing because of his own suffering.

We are not sure what illness the boy has. Many scholars feel it is epilepsy. This would fit the first description: "it seizes him, it dashes him down; and he foams and grinds his teeth and becomes rigid." The epilepsy hypothesis is also supported by the "dumb spirit" in the boy. A later description suggests a psychotic experience like that of the Gerasene demoniac: "it (the demon) has often cast him into the fire and into the water to destroy him." The illness is confusing, and most scholars believe this story to combine two healing stories in one. The descriptions of two illnesses are intertwined. There is also a discrepancy over the role of the crowd. In the beginning we hear that Jesus came upon a great crowd with his disciples arguing with the scribes. Later we hear that a crowd comes running together as Jesus drives out the unclean spirit, suggesting that he had been alone with father and son. Such mixing of stories is common in the Bible; in both the Old Testament and the gospels we commonly find two or more versions of the same story, or slightly different stories merged together. But whatever the actual illnesses, the healing approach is the same. A demon underlies the symptoms, and Jesus addresses himself to it.

When the boy is brought to Jesus, the spirit in the boy sees Jesus and convulses the boy. Once again, a negative spirit reacts strongly to a healing presence. Encountering the healer, the activity of the unclean spirit becomes magnified. Its pain increases. In psychotherapy we call this the phenomenon of resistance. The unclean spirits in us do not let themselves be driven out without a fight. They want to have their way. They make a big commotion in hopes that we will be frightened off and not deal with them. This particular demon, while making it more painful for the young man and his father, does not frighten the healer, Jesus.

Since the boy has a dumb spirit and Jesus cannot talk directly with it, he talks with the boy's father instead. He does a quick case history, asking how long the boy has had this condition. The father answers that the condition has lasted from childhood and that the spirit "has often cast him into the fire and into the water." This is valuable data, for both fire and water have profound symbolic meaning throughout the Bible, as well as in dreams and other experiences of the inner life. From Moses at the burning bush to the tongues of fire at Pentecost, fire symbolizes the presence of the Spirit of God. From the story of creation to the passage through the Red Sea, to Jesus' baptism, water represents new life and the source of all life. Possibly this spirit did not intend to destroy the boy, as the father feared, but to transform him. They needed someone to understand and help with the process. Often the fantasies of a person, even a psychotic, contain hints of the meaning and purpose needed to bring healing. So too, compulsive behaviors and the psychological aspects of our physical distress contain the seeds of God's transformation and healing.

As the man relates his son's history, he is overcome. He beseeches Jesus to do something. "If you can do anything, have pity on us and help us." The man is distraught and frustrated, unsure if healing is possible. He would desperately like Jesus to do something. In his pain and fear, he puts too much responsibility on Jesus: "If *you* can." Jesus indicates to the man that healing is certainly possible, and if *he* believes, he carries some of the power to make it happen. Healing is not just up to Jesus, but to the man as well. Jesus perceives that this man's faith is undeveloped. The man immediately responds, "I believe; help my unbelief!" He accepts Jesus' perception and expresses willingness to work on his undeveloped spiritual life. He is willing to grow in faith and in understanding the ways of God.

The man's statement indicates he has some faith, some belief. If he had none, he would not have gone to all this trouble to seek healing for his son. He still has lingering doubts, however, and they have to be dispelled for his son to be healed. The problem of the boy's being thrown into the fire and the water by this spirit is also the father's problem. The father must throw himself into the spiritual depths that the fire and water represent. His journey of faith and direct relationship with God must deepen. Devotion and love for his son lead him to recognize the spiritual gaps in his own life. This acknowledgement contributes to his son's healing.

In psychotherapy, the real transformation often begins when a person recognizes he is wounded or undeveloped. We see a similar pattern in this story. When this man recognizes his need for development, Jesus can bring healing to his son. Having explored the family situation, Jesus is now able to address the spirit, which had been unreachable for dialogue. He commands the deaf and dumb spirit to come out of the boy and never return. The spirit now hears and talks, for as soon as Jesus speaks it cries out in response. It convulses the boy and leaves him like a corpse, so that people think he is dead. As we have seen in other cases, the demon or unclean spirit does not leave without a struggle, without one last attempt to sap the true life of its victim.

The final part of this story addresses the disciples' earlier inability to heal this boy. Privately they ask Jesus why they could not heal him, why they could not cast out this particular demon. Jesus' response suggests the depths required of agents of healing: "This kind cannot be driven out by anything but prayer." "Prayer" in the gospels refers to the deepest aspects of the spiritual life. It expresses much more than the general forms of prayer talked about in our times. Jesus could heal this man because he had made the deepest possible contact with the inner spiritual world, a contact represented in the synoptic gospels by the forty days in the wilderness. There, Mark tells us, Jesus was tempted by Satan, was with the wild beasts, and was ministered to by angels. All three experiences depict encounters with the inner world or unconscious. The wild beasts represent the raw instinctive forces of the psyche as seen in dreams and fantasies. Their appearance often prefigures a healthy connection to nature and potential for healing. Satan is the inner voice that seduces one away from God's purposes. (Matthew and Luke develop further this part of Jesus' encounter in the wilderness.) The appearance of the angels indicates Jesus' success in these struggles and the guidance he received from God.

The disciples could not heal this man because they had not yet had this kind of inner encounter, as Jesus makes clear in rebuking Peter at Caesarea Philippi (Mk 8:31–33). Peter does not understand the mysterious workings of God and has become a voice for Satan, that which opposes

God's purposes. The transfiguration follows this dialogue and supports Jesus for avoiding Satan's trap. It reiterates to the bumbling Peter that Jesus is indeed speaking of the ways of God. This healing story immediately follows the transfiguration, and the difference in spiritual development is augmented by the fact that Jesus can heal and the disciples cannot. When the healing is completed, Jesus speaks again with his disciples of his coming passion. They still do not understand him, but this time no one objects as Peter had done earlier (Mk 9:30–32).

If the disciples knew truly how to pray, how to enter the spiritual depths, they could have healed this boy. Similarly, they would have understood Jesus' response to his own passion. Oddly, it seems that as long as Jesus himself remained with them, such growth could never happen. They counted on him to create this kind of encounter for them, but they would not make it themselves. They remained too dependent on Jesus, like the man in our story at the outset. This created the sort of tension and frustration in Jesus that he indicated by exclaiming at the disciples' inability to cast out the demon in this boy: "O faithless generation, how long am I to be with you? How long am I to bear with you?" The man in the story is not the only one who needs a more developed faith and spiritual life. The disciples need it too. They too must be thrown into the fire and into the water of life.

He Casts Out Demons by the Prince of Demons

Even Jesus' opponents did not deny that he cast out demons. They challenged *how* he did so. Mark describes the debate in this way.

> Then he went home; and the crowd came together again, so that they could not even eat. And when his family heard it, they went out to seize him, for people were saying, "He is beside himself." And the scribes who came down from Jerusalem said, "He is possessed by Beelzebul, and by the prince of demons he casts out the demons." And he called them to him, and said to them in parables, "How can Satan cast out Satan? If a kingdom is divided against itself, that kingdom cannot stand. And if a house is divided against itself, that house will not be able to stand. And if Satan has risen up against himself and is divided, he cannot stand, but is coming to an end. But no one can enter a strong man's house and plunder his goods, unless he first binds the strong man; then indeed he may plunder his house.

"Truly, I say to you, all sins will be forgiven the sons of men, and whatever blasphemies they utter; but whoever blasphemes against the Holy Spirit never has forgiveness, but is guilty of an eternal sin"—for they had said, "He has an unclean spirit" (Mk 3:19b–30).[18]

Some people think Jesus is "beside himself," and the scribes from Jerusalem believe he is possessed by Beelzebul. They differ only to the degree they believe Jesus is possessed. The scribes believe that Jesus casts out demons by Beezebul. It is to their accusation that Jesus speaks.

Matthew and Luke omit these references, preferring not to deal with them. However, John develops the theme of possession in his gospel, referring to it more often even than Mark.[19] In John 8:49 Jesus specifically denies that he has a demon, and the people perceive that someone possessed by a demon could not heal. "These are not the sayings of one who has a demon. Can a demon open the eyes of the blind?" (Jn 10:21).

To Jesus, all healing must be the work of the Spirit. It is a sign of the presence of God. To be an agent of healing, one cannot be bound by a demon. This recalls what we have seen with shamanism. The shaman's first patient is always himself. By diminishing the influence of the complexes or unclean spirits in his own life, he becomes a better healing agent to others. If a therapist has not "worked through" his own unconscious complexes, he is much more likely to inflict them on others. Jesus never let himself get caught in the petty games of the scribes and Pharisees, which had nothing to do with healing. This is what he addresses in his statement about the unforgivable sin, the sin against the Holy Spirit. The Holy Spirit comes for the healing of each soul. To avoid or deny God's call to healing in ourselves or in others is the greatest sin. We can risk all manner of living as long as we seek to respond to the healing Spirit of God.

What is of a demon and what is of God ultimately depends on our connection to life. Jesus, a man led by the Spirit, was perceived by many as being possessed, as having a demon. To an untutored human consciousness, it is not easy to perceive which is which. In particular, we tend to label as demonic anything with which we human beings are not comfortable. Jesus made a lot of people uncomfortable. His healing frightened some people,[20] and as we shall see, it threatened the authority of others like the Pharisees. It took a special kind of person to be open to his healing power. Casting out demons, or even perceiving them correctly, is not an easy matter. Shamans spend years and years learning the nuances of the spiritual world. The person who has not made this inner encounter often falls into the mistake of labeling as demonic what is really of the Spirit, even in the name of the Spirit.

Our culture has a problem absent in the culture of Jesus. Most people today do not believe in demons, nor are they aware through experience of the forces within us, complexes and other unconscious contents, that influence our psychological and physical health. The gospels make it clear that a life in the Spirit is meant to help us perceive such things. All too often people today believe that if only they have the Spirit, they need not worry about other influences from within. But the more we deny or ignore them, the more they influence us. The more we allow the Spirit to guide us in recognizing inner demons and dealing with them creatively, the more we can lead a richer, fuller, more challenging spiritual life—a life of healing.

The gospels indicate further that "denominational" requirements are not important in a healing ministry. We hear this little story from Mark:

> John said to him, "Teacher, we saw a man casting out demons in your name, and we forbade him, because he was not following us." But Jesus said, "Do not forbid him; for no one who does mighty work in my name will be able soon after to speak evil of me. For he that is not against us is for us" (Mk 9:38–40).[21]

Jesus was not concerned with forming a cohesive religious group. He told the Gerasene demonic to stay behind, though the man wanted to follow him. Jesus is not upset, like the disciples, that this man who is casting out demons in his name should not be a member of their group. The man is doing healing work, and that is what matters. There is no indication that Jesus tries to influence him in any way. Rather, the incident serves as a lesson to the disciples, who are more concerned about their group than about true healing. Such actions often reveal an undeveloped consciousness. Individuals who are too identified with their group have not adequately developed their relationship with themselves and God.

Unfortunately, today's church often seems equally afraid of the healing arts that do not fall directly within institutional life. Once Norman Cousins told a group how he had overcome a life-threatening illness through personal means and was helping others to do the same.[22] Generally, these were people, like Cousins himself, whose medical prognosis was viewed as very bleak. Cousins showed that healing could still be found. The strongest reaction against him, expressed only after the open discussion, came from a clergyman with "theological" objections. Cousins' language, he said, wasn't "Christian" enough. This clergyman's "theology" blinded him to the healing value of Cousins' work. Healing of this kind furthers the work of Jesus. It serves God's purposes, whether or not we belong to a particular group or espouse any brand of faith.

Taking More Seriously the Casting Out of Demons

The gospel teaches that if we are able to be involved in a healing ministry, we do well to consider Jesus' work in casting out demons. The gospels, shamanistic healing, and Jung's psychology of the unconscious all help us in this effort. We all harbor demons that need to be driven out, psychological complexes and attitudes that impede the best vision and living of life. If we do not attend to them, become aware of them, they can lead to physical and psychological illnesses. Often in our society people believe they have dealt fully with something if they have grasped it intellectually and conceptually. But experience has shown time and again that many things are a matter of the heart and must be worked out on the deeper, feeling levels of our lives. Here, the casting out of demons can be experienced as quite real and sometimes even frightening. It is on this level that we see just how important this approach to life can be.

The stories we have discussed show that Jesus' casting out demons covers a broad spectrum.[23] At times the evangelists, especially Mark, have an interesting twist in their accounts. It is the demons who first recognize Jesus (though he instructs them not to make him known).[24] It is in the inner world that God's healing power is first felt and experienced, though usually it has not yet reached human consciousness. Examples are frequently seen in dreams. In the beginning of psychotherapy and at intervals during the process, dreams occur that indicate a person's potential for healing and development. At such points, however, the person is still unconscious of this potential. The dreams begin to make the person aware of this process and the direction it will be taking. Sometime later the person may realize the emerging energy and potential so that it becomes a living part of life.

For example, a middle-aged postman had been a sober alcoholic for six years. He came to therapy to work on his family and work relationships. As he put it, "There has to be more to life than just staying sober." Early in our work together he dreamed that he had been elected president of the local chapter of the postal workers' union. I asked what he thought of the dream. He thought it was silly—he would never be elected to any such position. At that time he wasn't active in the union. Listening to this man, I felt that the dream was showing his true potential, where the healing forces within him would lead. In the unconscious, in the world of spirits and demons, God's healing grace was already known and could be perceived. It was not yet available to human consciousness.

In the next two years a number of developments took place. In the first few months this man was asked to serve as editor of the union's newsletter. He accepted the job, at first doubting his abilities. As he worked, he came to enjoy it and turned out a good product. He proudly brought copies to our meetings. After a year he was asked to run for secretary of the local union. He accepted, ran, and was elected. During the next year he attended a national conference of union officials, which he thoroughly enjoyed. By the following year, he had come to an interesting crossroads. First, he indicated that if the current president of the union stepped down, he was considering running for that position. During his terms as newsletter editor and secretary he had realized that he could do as good a job as, if not better than, the current president. He was also being offered positions in management by the postal service. He would serve out his term as secretary and then decide. It was not until two years after his dream that he reached his inner potential for professional work. Yet the "spirit" in his unconscious had perceived it much earlier.

This man's experience is typical. People's dreams often indicate their potential for growth and healing long before these qualities become conscious. The early reaction of demons to the presence of Jesus shows the same principle at work. Awareness of the healing dynamic had not reached the people, including the disciples, who witnessed these events. God often has to rely on more dynamic events to get our attention. Psychological and physical illnesses and the host of personal crises that afflict human life can often be seen as God's attempt to draw our attention to what is going on within. Belief in God alone is not enough to draw our attention to his transforming power in us; we are reluctant to accept anything that threatens our present adaptation to life. Both the teachings of Jesus and modern depth psychology indicate that it is possible to discover the inner kingdom of heaven, if we are open to it, without a great crisis.[25]

The gospels make it clear that even though the disciples were not fully developed healers, they could nevertheless do some healing and casting out of demons on their own while Jesus was still with them.[26] Jesus intended that those who followed after him continue his work. We cannot dismiss it as something only for him and beyond our abilities. To do this work we must have the direct contact with the inner world necessary to carry out such a ministry and develop the necessary consciousness.

Given the nature of this side of human experience, it should not be surprising that Jesus tells us that such aspects of reality must be continually dealt with. Matthew and Luke record this story of an unclean spirit.

> When the unclean spirit has gone out of a man, he passes through waterless places seeking rest, but he finds none. Then he says, "I will return to my house from which I came." And when he comes he finds it empty, swept, and put in order. Then he goes and brings with him seven other spirits more evil than himself, and they enter and dwell there; and the last state of that man becomes worse than the first. So shall it be also with this evil generation (Mt 12:43–45).[27]

Demons and the like are not destroyed, but driven away. However, once they have been driven away, once the symptoms that have caused pain are removed, there is a danger that we will revert to our old ways, causing a deeper and more severe crisis. If we do not continually seek to fill ourselves with the healing spirit of God and a growing personality, the old demons, neurotic tendencies, and illnesses can return worse than ever. We are called to move forward creatively under the guidance of the Spirit. Once we touch the Spirit of God in healing, we have to be careful not to let it go. Or, as Jesus puts it, "no one who puts his hand to the plow and looks back is fit for the kingdom of God" (Lk 9:62).

In my own life and psychotherapeutic practice I have found the reality of unclean spirits or demons a helpful way to reflect on many human situations. Of course, such imagery and language can be grossly overdone and misused, as in the gospels when the Pharisees and others concluded that Jesus had a demon. In our own time this aspect of inner experience, generally forgotten, can be immeasurably valuable in facilitating healing. It also has special dangers in an age in which most people do not believe in demons and the like.

At the turn of the century, before there was any understanding of the psychoses, psychotic people were usually considered demon-possessed. Their behavior and hallucinations were not encompassed in the rationalism of that time, and thus they were dismissed. Jung was the only one to perceive meaning in the hallucinations of the severely mentally ill. He saw in them an attempt of the psyche to heal itself using the language of symbol and myth, found most readily in each of our dreams. He pointed out that these experiences of the severely mentally ill were threatening to modern people because they opened up a realm of experience that had been largely forgotten. Besides, these people seemed unable to relate to the day-to-day life of the majority of the population. Dismissing such experience as demonic or irrational avoids the creative healing life to be found therein. For less severe psychological illnesses and many physical illnesses it is the same.

The great value of a psychology like Jung's is that it provides a modern empirical base for healing that can include the notion of spiritual realities. It helps us see life in the broadest sense as Jesus did. Such realities influence our health and offer avenues of psychological development. They belonged to the healing ministry of Jesus, made shamanistic healing effective, and cannot be ignored today. They offer an important consideration for any healing ministry.

NOTES

[1] C.G. Jung, *Memories, Dreams, Reflections,* p. 177.

[2] Most relevant to this point is "Book the Second: Of the Dark Night of the Spirit," p. 91f.

[3] See C.G. Jung, *The Archetypes and the Collective Unconscious.*

[4] See John A. Sanford, *The Man Who Wrestled with God,* Chapters 1–3.

[5] Lk 8:2 and Mk 16:9.

[6] See C.G. Jung, *The Structures and Dynamics of the Psyche,* CW, Vol. 8, "A Review of the Complex Theory" and "The Psychological Foundations of Belief in Spirits." See also Vera Buhrmann's *Living in Two Worlds: Communication Between a White Healer and Her Black Counterparts.*

[7] See for example John W. Perry's "Jung and the New Approach to Psychosis" and *The Far Side of Madness.*

[8] John A. Sanford, *The Kingdom Within.*

[9] Mk 1:12–13; Mt 4:1–11; Lk 4:1–13.

[10] There is a subtle irony in this story. Elsewhere in his teachings Jesus says, "Do not throw your pearls before swine" (Mt 7:6), but with unclean spirits it is a very different matter.

[11] See the parable of the talents, Mt 25:14–30 and Lk 19:11–27.

[12] See Chapter 9.

[13] Frances Wickes, *The Inner World of Childhood.*

[14] For further reference see Robert Johnson, *He,* and John A. Sanford, *The Invisible Partners.*

[15] For further reference see Irene de Castillejo, *Knowing Woman,* and Sanford, *The Invisible Partners.*

[16] William P. Blatty, *The Exorcist.*

[17] Thomas J. Kapacinskas, "*The Exorcist* and the Spiritual Problem of Modern Woman."

[18] See also parallels in Matthew 12:22–30 and Luke 11:14–23. Matthew 9:32–34 and 10:25b repeat this theme.

[19] Jn 7:20, 8:48, 8:52, and 10:20.

[20] Mk 5:15. Recall our discussion of the healing of the Gerasene demoniac.

[21] See also parallel in Lk 9:49–50.

[22] Cousins, *Anatomy of an Illness,* Chapter 1.

[23] Other brief references to the healings of demoniacs include Mk 1:32–34 (parallels in Mt 8:16–17 and Lk 4:40–41), Mk 1:39, 3:11–12, Mt 4:24, Lk 6:18, and 13:31–32.

[24] See especially Mk 1:34 (parallel in Lk 4:41), Mk 3:11–12 (parallel in Mt 12:16), and Mk 1:23–27, discussed earlier in the chapter.

[25] John A. Sanford, *The Kingdom Within* and *Healing and Wholeness,* especially Chapter 4, the chapter on shamanism.

[26] See Mk 3:14–15; 6:7; 6:13; 16:17–18; Mt 10:1; 10:7–8; Lk 9:1–2; 10:9. These are discussed further in Chapter 12.

[27] See also Lk 11:24–26.

Chapter 4
Healing and Society

As we have seen, our society has forgotten avenues of healing that remain alive in other cultures, like that of the American Indian. It should come as no surprise that the life our society imposes on many of its members makes them ill, both physically and psychologically. Our culture's negative influence on our psychological health was first perceived by psychiatrists early in this century. More recently, health care professionals have discovered that problems of life in modern society contribute to physical illness as well. Doctors are becoming more aware of the psychogenic side of physical complaints.

Generally speaking, people in our society feel more comfortable dealing with physical ailments than with psychological ones. If they are physically ill, they believe a doctor will be able to cure the illness without their having to take responsibility for it. Yet, by some estimates, as much as ninety percent of all physical illness has a psychological component.[1] In other words, when the body is out of balance, it is a good indication that the soul is out of balance too. The soul may be in distress because of the climate it inhabits. Any illness, psychological or physical, may be an attempt by the soul to let us know that something is wrong.[2] The illness is not itself the problem, but an attempt to call our attention to an underlying dilemma. Something has gone wrong in the proper unfolding and fullest expression of an individual's personality.

We do not have to look far for evidence of this. For example, acutely psychotic people rarely develop cancer.[3] It is as if the inner turmoil erupts in a totally psychic way precluding major physical symptoms. Disharmony within ourselves is expressed both psychologically and physically. Modern doctors continually discover the connection between our psyche and such major disease threats as heart disease, cancer, respiratory disorders, arthritis, digestive disorders, and even viral infections.[4]

We can best see our society's role in such disorders and illnesses by considering the concept of stress.[5] The more complex society becomes, the more stress it generates, as evidenced by our crowded cities, the complexities of modern finance, even the rush of the Christmas season. Society also prepares us inadequately for experiences of normal living, such as human relationships and death. Such factors affect our health. Usually we find

either drugs or psychological techniques to alleviate many of the symptoms. But they do not get us to the bottom of the problem. We continue
to live burdened by an unbalanced society, out of tune with the natural
drive for health that lies within each of us. This is the approach presented by Jesus in the gospels. We become healthy and live the life God
intends when we live out of the true self we are intended to become.
This will not be dictated or mediated by society, but by God and his
healing within us.

Certain of the gospel healing stories revolve around social acceptance
and society's role in healing and illness. A good place to begin is with the
story of the blind man we discussed earlier.[6] Mark tells us that "some
people" brought this man to Jesus. Only a few seem to care enough about
healing this man to lead him to Jesus. They believe he can see. Then Jesus
"took the blind man by the hand, and led him out of the village." Jesus
prefers to do his work in private, for the sake of healing itself, and not in
public, to gain personal recognition. This is one reason he leads the man
out of the village. The other is that the atmosphere in the village has been
responsible for the man's being ill. At the end of the story, Jesus sends him
home, saying, "Do not even enter the village."

Freud is said to have remarked that he could have been far more
successful with his patients if he had not had to send them back to the
family or social situation that made them sick to begin with. Families, social
groups, religious groups, and whole societies can have a strong negative
influence on the health of certain of their members. Usually such individuals are ostracized simply because they are different. As a result, they
become ill and are rejected further. Such individuals are valued not for
themselves, but only for being dutiful, "appropriate" members of the
group. But for many, such conformity means psychological or physical
illness and the violation of their God-given personality.

Mark's account of the blind man shows how the individual personality
unfolds in a collective atmosphere. "Some people"—one or more—care
enough about a person to prepare the way. They were not capable of *doing*
the healing, but they could lead the man in the right direction. From there
it was up to him and Jesus. If the man had chosen to return to the town,
despite Jesus' instructions, all might have been lost. The story makes the
point that God cares for each individual as a unique self, not just as part of
a group. God can be experienced if even a few people are concerned
enough to lead a person to the source of healing. This may mean giving up
old relationships in favor of more healing ones.

Another story that emphasizes the personal nature of healing versus a more collective one concerns a deaf man with a speech impediment.

> Then he returned from the region of Tyre, and went through Sidon to the Sea of Galilee, through the region of the Decapolis. And they brought to him a man who was deaf and had an impediment in his speech; and they besought him to lay his hand upon him. And taking him aside from the multitude privately, he put his fingers into his ears, and he spat and touched his tongue; and looking up to heaven, he sighed, and said to him, "Eph-phatha," that is, "Be opened." And his ears were opened, his tongue was released, and he spoke plainly. And he charged them to tell no one; but the more he charged them, the more zealously they proclaimed it. And they were astonished beyond measure, saying, "He has done all things well; he even makes the deaf hear and the dumb speak" (Mk 7:31–37).

We observe in this healing some of the shamanistic actions of Jesus. He puts his fingers in the man's ears and spits and touches his tongue. We see the use of spittle, as well as direct contact with the impaired areas. Before Jesus takes these actions, he leads the man away privately. It seems that if the man is to be healed, he must be removed from the influence of the multitude. If he is to hear the things it is important for him to hear, and speak those things it is important for him to speak, then he must come into contact with the source of healing. Both personal contact with the healer and withdrawal from the collective influence are essential to the healing process. Similarly, in psychotherapy, two people meet for an hour away from other influences, holding those influences at a distance so that the client can begin to discover his true nature.

This aspect of this man's healing is brought out further by the interest-ing conclusion. Mark tells us that the man's ears are opened, his tongue is released, and he speaks plainly. Then Jesus charges the multitude to tell no one—but the more he charges them, the more zealously they proclaim it. The multitude proclaims what happened, but they do not "hear." They are incapable of following spiritual instructions. The man who was deaf can now hear, but the multitude does not. While he hears, they remain spiri-tually deaf.

Jesus had instructed the Gerasene demonic to talk of his own experi-ence. The crowd in this story is talking about the formerly deaf man's experience. They are not talking about their own experience, however. There has been no personal transformation in them, physical or spiritual, that would give them anything to talk about. They are living vicariously through this man and through Jesus, but not in themselves. From this perspective it is quite understandable why Jesus did not want them to say anything about what had happened. He was not interested in developing a public reputation, but in the genuine transformation and healing of body and soul. So as the story ends, not only does the man hear and the multitude remain spiritually deaf, but he now speaks plainly, while what they proclaim is spiritual folly.

The accounts of the healing of leprosy in the gospels also reveal an underlying social dilemma in the afflicted person. We find such a story early in the gospel of Mark.

> And a leper came to him beseeching him, and kneeling said to him, "If you will, you can make me clean." Moved with pity, he stretched out his hand and touched him, and said to him, "I will; be clean." And immediately the leprosy left him, and he was made clean. And he sternly charged him, and sent him away at once, and said to him, "See that you say nothing to anyone, but go, show yourself to the priest, and offer for your cleansing what Moses commanded, for a proof to the people." But he went out and began to talk freely about it, and to spread the news, so that Jesus could no longer openly enter a town, but was out in the country; and people came to him from every quarter (Mk 1:40–45).[7]

The man who comes to Jesus here makes an interesting entreaty. "If you will, you can make me clean." Mark tells us that he has a beseeching attitude and kneels before Jesus while making his plea. The man shows a desire to be healed and a belief that Jesus can heal him, if he is willing. Like the father of the boy with the dumb spirit, he puts the onus on Jesus. Most interesting is his request to be made "clean." The reference is not to his illness, but to this state of rejection it has left him in. Leprosy and certain other skin diseases were not acceptable in Judaism under the levitical code. Because of this disease, this man was considered ritually unclean. His strongest desire was not to be rid of the leprosy, but to be rid of the social rejection, the isolation. Jesus understands and responds accordingly—"moved with pity," according to Mark, but "pity" does not convey the meaning of the original. The Greek *splagchnistheis* is a derivative of a word that refers to a person's bowels, the deepest seat of the emotions. Jesus' response is thus a profoundly emotional one, better described as deep compassion. Jesus felt not only the man's physical ills, but his social rejection. He could not help responding to this man's condition. He answers, "I will; be clean."

It is worth noticing Jesus' specific actions here. "He stretched out his hand and touched him." Jesus does not always touch the people he heals, but this man's social isolation required personal contact. No one would have any direct contact with him, and he needed this approach. Scholars tell us that the man's disease was not necessarily leprosy. It could have been any skin ailment that did not meet the ritual requirements found in Leviticus 14. Many skin ailments carry psychosomatic implications—that there is "something under one's skin," for instance, something just under the surface that wants to come out, a part of the person that has not been accepted and cannot emerge. Jesus' touching this man is a deep act of acceptance: to heal this leper Jesus must break the rules that have isolated him from the rest of society.

Jesus concludes this encounter with the stern charge, "See that you say nothing to anyone; but go, show yourself to the priest, and offer for your cleansing what Moses commanded, for a proof to the people." These instructions show that Jesus understood fully the society's ritual requirements for reconciliation. His instructions remind the man of what he must do to become ritually clean. Only the priest can officially certify him as clean and make him socially acceptable once again.

A strange thing happens on the man's way to the priest. The man does not follow Jesus' instructions, but instead goes out and talks freely about what has happened to him. Jesus' reputation grows and he can no longer enter towns openly. The man is doing exactly what Jesus suggested the Gerasene demoniac do but with subtle differences. Jesus specifically sent the demoniac to his friends whereas this man is acting on his own and ignoring Jesus' instructions. The leper's action results from both an inner transformation and an inclination to get carried away with himself. Whereas he had been very eager to be reconciled with his society, now he does not seem to care at all. He does not follow through on his responsibility in the healing process.

Jesus sought to help the leper become reconciled to his society as well as to heal the disease. To heal him Jesus broke society's rules but he never completely cut himself off from its customs and practices without good reason. We hear, for example, that he paid taxes and respected the need for a social order. Jesus recognized the tension between the health of an individual and the demands of society. The man who came to Jesus was probably ill because of just such tension. He had struggled hard to fulfill society's dictates, but something in him suffered, something in him was denied. Something was under his skin. Since he had not come to grips with the part of himself that did not fit society's standards, he came down with an illness that put him in the very situation he did not want to face. Psychologically, we might say that he left certain parts of his personality in his unconscious in his attempts to fulfill society's norms. The result: illness.

Even if the man actually had leprosy, the same parallel can be made. Leprosy is a disease that affects the nerve endings and blocks the normal signals of pain that alert the body to a threatening situation.[8] If this man had leprosy, it may have been a psychosomatic symptom of his psychological situation. Since he was not able to experience the natural tension between himself and society, he experienced it as bodily illness. The particular illness, as we have seen, forced him to face the psychological tension he was avoiding.

In psychotherapy, the majority of patients experience some conflict between conscious expression of their true personality and external demands conveyed through family, school, church, and society as a whole. For no one do the parables of the lost sheep and the lost coin have more meaning than for the many individuals who, if they deny part of their personality, become ill.[9] Such aspects of human nature often include much of our feeling life, sexuality, and the thoughts and fantasies that lead a person beyond the general level of collective thinking. If such feelings and thoughts can be integrated into the personality, then a person can live more creatively. If not, then psychological or physical illness may result, and at best the person lives a mundane and nondescript existence. The life Jesus calls us to live is not meant to be mundane, but full and creative.

Accompanying the cure of the leper is a growth in personal consciousness. In being healed, the man so eager to be reconciled to society now no longer cares about fulfilling the necessary requirements. The cure is effected by Jesus' healing action toward the man, in particular his total acceptance of him, an acceptance he could not procure from society with its regulations. When the man is cured, he senses why. Because Jesus' actions toward him surpass the cultural norm, he is able to discover the unacceptable part of himself, and express it. Good psychotherapy provides just such acceptance, enabling individuals to embrace aspects of their personality that they had not experienced before.

We can certainly appreciate this man's enthusiasm for his healing experience. We can understand why he wanted to tell people what Jesus had done. But we also have to remember Jesus' very specific instructions: "See that you say nothing to anyone; but go, show yourself to the priest, and offer for your cleansing what Moses commanded, for a proof to the people." By going off and speaking freely, the former leper ignored Jesus' instructions. It is important that we consider what Jesus had in mind with his admonitions. To begin with, Jesus has instructed the man not to say anything to anyone. It is important that he be silent, that he not follow his first inclination to run out and tell everyone. Jesus is suggesting to this man that he needs to temper his enthusiasm and understand the healing he has received.

We saw earlier that Jesus went into the wilderness after his baptism to wrestle with Satan and put his baptism into perspective. Jesus perceives a need for this man to do likewise. Ironically, just when the man discovers his inner conflict with society, Jesus prescribes one of society's ritual requirements. Because of the cure, the man has fallen into a psychological state opposite to the one he had been in before: once very concerned about being a respectable member of society, he now no longer cares a bit for its customs or rituals. Jesus seeks to help the man achieve the balance that Jesus himself lives out. While he often argued with the pillars of his own society—the scribes and Pharisees—Jesus participated regularly in the customs of both synagogue and temple. Here he attempts to show this man the way to a similar balance between the twin dangers, on the one hand, of slavish adherence to the customs and laws of society, with the resulting denial of parts of himself, and, on the other hand, of excessive withdrawal from society, leading to spiritual inflation and other difficulties.

Soon after the event, we hear that this man has made it awkward for Jesus to get about openly and thus limited his movement. His overboard response has hurt the person who healed him. By sending this man to the priest, Jesus hoped to have him attain a proper internal balance. Only then could he live conscious of the tension between himself and the societal structure, and he would not try to identify one-sidedly with what society required. This man missed an opportunity to grow psychologically and spiritually. He received the cure, but missed the spiritual lesson that came with it. In psychotherapy, some people hope to overcome a specific problem or life dilemma. When the problem is overcome, they return to life much as they lived it before. In some cases, they do as this man did and switch to a completely opposite lifestyle. Others, as they work on the original problem, begin to see it as something that calls for further growth and development. They move beyond eliminating the symptom to follow a new life path. Such a path recognizes both individual uniqueness and the responsibility to be a creative member of society.

Illness can often be seen as an attempt to call a person into proper creative tension with society. Healing indicates that we are called to be creative individuals within our societies, not just adapted ones.[10]

Jesus' healing ministry draws our attention to subtle aspects of life beyond the mere keeping of rules, customs, mores, and other explicit and implicit regulations. Often a fragile relationship exists between individuals and society. For this reason Jesus admonishes us, "Unless your righteousness exceeds that of the scribes and the Pharisees, you will never enter the kingdom of heaven" (Mt 5:20). It was the "righteousness" of the scribes and the Pharisees that made this man ill, and could not heal him. Hard as it is to live the disciplined life of a scribe or a Pharisee, it is not enough, if we are going to bring healing to others and have the spiritual awareness that comes with it.

One other healing story in the gospels involves leprosy. It is the story of ten lepers, found only in Luke's gospel:

> On the way to Jerusalem he was passing along between Samaria and Galilee. And as he entered a village, he was met by ten lepers, who stood at a distance and lifted up their voices and said, "Jesus, Master, have mercy on us." When he saw them he said to them, "Go and show yourselves to the priests." And as they went they were cleansed. Then one of them, when he saw that he was healed, turned back, praising God with a loud voice; and he fell on his face at Jesus' feet, giving him thanks. Now he was a Samaritan. Then said Jesus, "Were not ten cleansed? Where are the nine? Was no one found to return and give praise to God except this foreigner?" And he said to him, "Rise and go your way; your faith has made you well" (Lk 17:11–19).

Here Luke builds on the theme from Mark concerning the healing of a leper. We have seen that Jesus healed people individually and that this story of the healing of ten lepers is not factually accurate. Luke uses it to make important points. Ten lepers approach Jesus from a distance and ask for help. Jesus sends them to the priests. This story omits the important interaction in the beginning of Mark's story. What matters most to Luke is the ending. The ten lepers head directly to the priests. On the way they are healed; their faith in the cure prescribed by Jesus brings the healing they sought. Here the story takes a new twist. One of the men, seeing he is healed, returns to Jesus praising God and falls on his face at Jesus' feet giving thanks. The other nine, presumably, continue on their way as instructed, present themselves to the priests, are declared clean, and return to their previous lives. Cured, they can fit back into society.

Luke tells us that the man who returned to Jesus was a Samaritan. (Only Luke's gospel [10:25–37] has the parable of the good Samaritan.) Samaritans were not bound by the rules and regulations of the Jerusalem temple; they were looked down upon by the Jews, whose faith was rooted in temple worship. The Samaritans based their faith on ancient traditions handed down through Moses: centering their worship around Mount Gerizim and the area surrounding it, they claimed descent from the remnant left after the exile of the kingdoms of Israel. The Jews in Judea claimed the Samaritans were descended from colonists deported into Samaria by the Assyrians, who had adopted an inferior version of the cult of the Israelite God. Consequently, the Judeans would have nothing to do with them.

In Luke's story the leprosy shared by these ten men brought them together in a most unusual way. Luke shows us, as did Mark, the power of the social stigma of the disease. Ostracized as they were, it did not matter that the Judeans kept company with a Samaritan. Their illness brought about a special kind of fellowship. The healing of the nine does not bring about any real transformation, however. They will be accepted by the priests and resume their old lives, no longer having anything to do with the Samaritans. The Samaritan, on the other hand, sees something happening in him that is worth a personal response, not just a conventional one. He has no stake in being ritually clean, so he returns to Jesus to make his response and to give thanks for what has happened. This man's healing has brought him into deeper relationship with God. He does not succumb, like the others, to being a faithful member of the society that had ostracized him. Jesus appears to support this man's actions when he wonders aloud why the others have not returned: "Was no one found to return and give praise to God except this foreigner?" However low his social status, the Samaritan has made an appropriate personal response to God.

Jesus dismisses him with words as heartfelt as any that appear in the gospels to those who have not only been cured of an illness but transformed psychologically and spiritually as well: "Rise and go your way; your faith has made you well." This statement is so crucial to an understanding of Jesus' healing that we will return to it later. Suffice it to say that it is a deeply supportive act on Jesus' part.

Luke tells this story to contrast the levels of spiritual transformation that can ensue from the cure of an illness. Nine of the ten people will accept the cure and try to resume life exactly as before. They take the cure for granted. And it is the same today. People have very high expectations of their doctors. They believe that healing is their right, not a gift from God. They want their symptoms removed so that they can go right back to the life they have been living. In such cases, no inner healing takes place, and life is not lived in a new and deeper way.

One in ten times, people are so touched by the healing (and the illness) that they look for God in it and try to understand their experience. They emerge filled with new purpose and meaning, ready to live life more fully and richly. Inner healing and transformation take place because the person is *responding* to the source of healing, God. Luke implies that the main reason this happened to this man was that he was a Samaritan, unacceptable to the larger society. Because he was not bound by the customs of this society, the Samaritan was free to respond to Jesus and to God in his own way.

Luke's presentation—nine men who return to Jerusalem for ritual cleansing and a Samaritan who makes a personal response to God—hints at another important aspect of healing. The nine and the one had different religious orientations and backgrounds. Religion influenced their response to their healing. What is the relationship between religion and healing? When does religion get in the way of healing or even cause illness, and when is it an agent of healing and health? A number of the gospel healing stories address this issue, and it is to them we now turn.

NOTES

[1] Cousins, *Anatomy of an Illness,* p. 55.

[2] John A. Sanford, "Interview with John Sanford," with Phyllis Mather Rice.

[3] Sanford, *Dreams and Healing,* p. 35.

[4] James Lynch, M.D., *The Broken Heart.* O. Carl Simonton, Stephanie

Matthews-Simonton, James Creighton, *Getting Well Again*. Kenneth R. Pelletier, *Mind as Healer, Mind as Slayer*. Bernie S. Siegel, *Love, Medicine & Miracles*.

[5] Hans Selye, M.D., *The Stress of Life*.
[6] Mk 8:22–26. See Chapter 2.
[7] Parallels are found in Matthew 8:1–4 and Luke 5:12–16.
[8] Cousins, Chapter 4.
[9] Lk 15:3–10 (also Mt 18:12–14).
[10] Sanford, *Healing and Wholeness,* Chapter 1.

Chapter 5
Healing and Religion

In sickness or danger, human beings have a deep instinct to turn to God. Primitive tribes, we have seen, have a shaman or religious healer, whom people consult when they need healing. Christian missionaries report that natives in foreign lands come to them for healing, not to the medical people. For the natives the religious figure offered the most potential for healing.[1] Likewise, in physical or psychological crisis, many people in our culture move in a religious direction. The clergy are very frequently consulted professionals. People who defy medical expectations to recover from life-threatening diseases commonly express a deepened sense of the religious, though not always in an orthodox sense. They often report spending part of each day in prayer, meditation, or quiet.[2] Alcoholics Anonymous, the most successful of any program treating alcoholism, takes essentially a religious approach; the AA Twelve Steps make a good foundation for any person's spiritual life.

Despite all this, by and large the church relegates its healing ministry to other professionals, medical and psychological. Most clergy and lay people limit their role to visitation, support, and prayer. The church usually does not see itself as part of the healing team. It has lost the vitality of Jesus' healing ministry, through which a living religious presence brings health and healing. Our society and the church seem to share the assumption that religion and health are not connected; body and soul are separate. Thus, if healing comes to the body through religious means, it is only through divine intervention. Jesus presents a different view: to him, healing was often close at hand. People simply had to search for it.

Parallels exist between our society and that of Jesus' day. Healing had not been part of Old Testament tradition, nor was it part of the religion of the scribes and the Pharisees. Even so those who came to Jesus for healing were responding to instincts deep in their souls. Through this religious man, they believed, they could find healing. Some, like the woman with the flow of blood,[3] had consulted many physicians. Others, like the lepers, had been rejected by their society, including the scribes and Pharisees, and had nowhere else to go.

Jesus' radical difference in attitude is best shown in the stories of healing in the synagogues. People came to the synagogues because something told them transformation could come from God. Unfortunately, as long as the synagogues remained under the sway of the scribes and Pharisees, they could not receive this transformation. But Jesus does heal these people, and in so doing he unveils deficiencies in the religion and the religious leaders of his day. One story we have already reviewed sets the stage, the healing of the man with an unclean spirit (Mk 1:23–27).[4] How ironic that a man with an unclean spirit should be found in the synagogue on the sabbath. The unclean spirit seemed perfectly content and quiet until Jesus arrived, but Jesus brought a higher consciousness, forcing the demon to be perceived and driven out. As this happens, the people recognize a new level of teaching. The synagogue now becomes a forum for the differences between Jesus and the Pharisees, between one religious approach that heals and another that does not.

The gospel story that makes this point most dramatically tells of the man with a withered hand.

> Again he entered the synagogue, and a man was there who had a withered hand. And they watched him, to see whether he would heal him on the sabbath, so that they might accuse him. And he said to the man who had the withered hand, "Come here." And he said to them, "Is it lawful on the sabbath to do good or to do harm, to save life or to kill?" But they were silent. And he looked around at them with anger, grieved at their hardness of heart, and said to the man, "Stretch out your hand." He stretched it out, and his hand was restored. The Pharisees went out, and immediately held counsel with the Herodians against him, how to destroy him (Mk 3:1–6).[5]

This story sets up the antagonism between Jesus and the Pharisees that recurs throughout the gospels. Jesus enters the synagogue and finds a man who needs healing. Mark tells us that the Pharisees watched to see if Jesus would heal on the sabbath. They considered it unlawful and therefore sinful to work on this day, and they took every opportunity to make their point. In the passage preceding this healing story,[6] for instance, Jesus' disciples are picking grain on the sabbath. Jesus reminds the outraged Pharisees that David ate the sacred bread reserved for the priests, and gave some to his hungry companions. David foregoes religious law to meet important human needs.

The Pharisees watch Jesus for all the wrong reasons. They could be watching to learn about healing. They could be watching to learn new meaning for the sabbath. But the Pharisees believe they know everything there is to know about the sabbath, and they believe that healing is not as important as their religious regulations. They are watching Jesus in order to accuse him. Their posture is dogmatic and hostile, defensive and self-righteous. Jesus threatens them, so they try to discredit him.

The setting itself is dramatic. The synagogue and the sabbath are the primary territory of the Pharisees. They dictate what goes on there and how everyone should act. But the synagogue is also the house of God, and the sabbath is the Lord's day. So, despite the Pharisees, Jesus finds a man in the synagogue whose instincts tell him that healing can come from a religious direction.

Clearly, Jesus senses all that is going on. He knows that God wants him to heal, so there is no way to avoid the accusations of the Pharisees. Jesus calls the man with the withered hand to him. They stand together in the midst of the Pharisees and all others gathered there. Then he addresses the Pharisees: "Is it lawful on the sabbath to do good or to do harm, to save life or to kill?" The question is a remarkable one, typical of Jesus' style of dialogue. On the surface the answer would seem very obvious: of course it is lawful on the sabbath to do good and to save life and not to do harm or to kill. Any child knows the answer. Jesus does not ask the question to arrive at a more precise theological definition of the sabbath. He asks it so that the Pharisees might recognize their unconscious hypocrisy and become more conscious of their true nature. As long as they deny this side of themselves, they will not understand Jesus' teaching or his healing. They badly need self-confrontation, and Jesus knows it. The Pharisees are in the synagogue on the sabbath, plotting to accuse Jesus and even do away with him. In other words, these pillars of the religious community are inwardly seeking to harm and maybe kill. Even a child should recognize that *they* are breaking the sabbath despite all their self-righteousness.

Nothing is more crucial for Jesus than understanding this aspect of spiritual life. Many of his teaching statements, his "woes to the Pharisees," address this problem. He shows them to be like whitewashed tombs. They pay attention only to the outside of the cup, neglect the inside, and by doing so shut off the kingdom of heaven, neither entering themselves, nor allowing those who might enter to do so.[7] For the Pharisees to understand Jesus, they must let go of their defensiveness and inclination to entrap him. They must do some very honest self-examination. The Pharisees lack any real wilderness experience. They have not come to grips with their own desire for power and self-righteousness. They have fallen prey to the temptations of Satan that Jesus so carefully avoided. Jesus confronts them with something in themselves of which they are unaware. The Pharisees are concerned above all with protecting their status as religious leaders. Thus, when Jesus reveals their spiritual inadequacies, they become preoccupied with self-justification. To Jesus, the synagogue and the sabbath offer an arena for self-awareness and healing; the Pharisees use this forum to support their self-righteousness.

The Pharisees lived an apparently spiritual life and taught others to live it by following prescribed codes. Jesus sees such a life as too extreme, denying important aspects of religion. In terms of his ministry, it was healing and the inner nature of men and women. Primitive shamans had no code of behavior or peculiar lifestyles. They were recognized for their healing and their contact with the inner world of spirits, but not for any particular lifestyle different from that of other people.[8] Jesus, likewise, did not set himself apart, but ate and drank with rich and poor alike, sinner and Pharisee. The Pharisees thought he was totally out of line, a glutton and a drunkard.[9]

To Jesus it was the Pharisees who were peculiar. They could not honestly perceive themselves and others. From the point of view of modern psychology, we would say that the Pharisees had a big "shadow problem." Trying to adhere to their strict religious codes, they left a large part of their personalities in the unconscious. When we deny parts of ourselves in this way, those parts become dangerous to us. Emotions repressed for whatever reasons can bring on illness, physical and psychological. Or we relieve ourselves of our unconscious shadows by projecting them onto others. The Pharisees projected their shadows onto those they judged, tax collectors and sinners. In so doing, they separated themselves from them. The Pharisees likewise projected their shadows onto Jesus, who challenged their hypocrisy and their resistance to self-awareness. They accused Jesus of blasphemy, of claiming to be God. Yet in the gospels, especially the more historical synoptics, Jesus makes no such claim. He teaches of God's kingdom. He judges no one. The Pharisees are the ones truly guilty of blasphemy, of playing God. Many Christians like to say that Jesus died for our sins. More accurately, he died because of the sin of the Pharisees, an element of human nature found in all of us. They lacked the inner experience to correct their own problem.

The opportunity for transformation exists in anyone. Jesus' question to the Pharisees gives them such an opportunity. With the right response they could have grown in self-awareness. Mark tells us that after Jesus asks his questions they are silent. Jesus' question had hit the mark. Great tension was in the air. It was a unique chance for growth. Yet while the silence indicates Jesus had touched something in the Pharisees, they remain unwilling to deal with the situation. In psychological terms, we would say they chose to leave the matter in the unconscious and not face it. By keeping silent they let the problem fester. In such cases it is only through interaction with another about the difficulty that we bring it out in the open. Jesus could get nowhere with the Pharisees, and so he turns his attention to the man with the withered hand.

As he addresses this man, it is important to note Jesus' emotional state. Earlier, at the healing of the leper, we saw Jesus filled with compassion (*splagchnistheis*). Now we see a very different emotional state. Mark tells us that he looked at the Pharisees with anger, grieved at their hardness of heart. In modern medical practice, such emotion would be considered most inappropriate. Who would care to have a surgeon operate just after finishing an angry, emotional debate with a colleague? Here is a very important difference between medical science and shamanistic healing. The medical doctor is expected to be cool and objective, but the shaman may be full of emotion. Depth psychology shows that our emotions connect us to the inner archetypal world and clarify our relationship to it. Emotions are not something to be shunned, but to be noted carefully and expressed creatively. They are one of our best links to our unconscious inner life.

Jesus was at home with his emotions. He did not try to avoid them. His anger is there, but it does not interfere with healing the man with the withered hand. Very likely it helped. Jesus was angry at the Pharisees because of their religious narrow mindedness, their hardness of heart. "Heart" in the biblical sense can be seen as a euphemism for the unconscious, the core of our emotional and feeling life. It had become constricted in their legalism. They could not develop what depth psychology calls the feeling function.[10] The feeling function is one of four primary psychological functions; it allows us to see the value of things and evaluates the data of experience very differently from its thinking counterpart.

This story contrasts the developed feeling function of Jesus with the undeveloped feeling of the Pharisees. To Jesus, the healing of the individual mattered far more than rules and regulations, which come from man and not from God. The Pharisees, because of their hardness of heart, could not let go of their attachment to rules. They could not discover the deeper values of life.

The problem of the heart is not limited to any time or culture. Carl Jung once traveled to America and visited with a Taos Pueblo medicine man, Ochwiay Biano, "Mountain Lake." While they talked of their two cultures, this Indian shaman said an interesting thing. "We think that they (the whites) are mad." Jung asked why. "They say that they think with their heads." "Why, of course. What do you think with?" Jung replied. "We think here," the Indian said, indicating his heart.[11] A life centered in the thinking of the heart is connected to the deeper dimension of being, which can bring healing as Jesus or any shaman does. It is significant that the greatest killer in our culture is heart disease. Since we are vulnerable here spiritually and psychologically, it seems we are vulnerable here physically as well.[12]

Jesus now gives a simple command to the man with the withered hand: "Stretch out your hand." Mark tells us that the man stretched it out, and his hand was restored. The general reading of this line is that Jesus tells the man to stretch out his hand, and as he does so the hand is healed. This is certainly a very dramatic image and an understandably popular one. But a slightly different image seems in keeping with the flow of the story. When the man raises his hand, the hand is *already* healed. Jesus asks him to raise it not to heal the hand, but to show the Pharisees what has happened while they have been talking. While the Pharisees have rejected the new consciousness offered by Jesus, this man has understood.

This man's condition was psychosomatic, and directly related to the spiritual state of the synagogue. Earlier, this problem was seen as an unclean spirit. Now it appears as a bodily symptom. Something needs to be "grasped" in this synagogue that is not being grasped. Both a physical and a spiritual problem exist. The man with the withered hand was ill because he had not yet "grasped" the situation. Jesus enters the synagogue and immediately perceives what is going on. He sees the hypocrisy and hardness of heart of the Pharisees. He offers the same opportunity to the Pharisees—to become conscious of the hypocrisy—that he offers the man with the withered hand. We recall that the Pharisees were watching Jesus in order to entrap him. Jesus, fully aware of their intentions, questions them about the sabbath. But first he calls the man with the withered hand to him. Thus, as Jesus asked his questions, the man is with him in the midst of the room. The question about the sabbath is directed not just to the Pharisees, but to him as well. Unlike the Pharisees, he comes to understand the true nature of the sabbath.

This man's religious instinct has led him to the synagogue on the sabbath for healing and connection with God. But to see and experience God's intention for healing, he also had to see the unconscious intentions of the Pharisees, their hypocrisy and hardness of heart. He had to grasp this in order to be freed from the atmosphere permeating the synagogue. Jesus' question allowed this man to perceive what was really going on. When Jesus offered a new level of consciousness the hand was healed. The evidence is now before the Pharisees. They can accept the restored hand as a sign that they need further religious development, or they can judge it as work and condemn Jesus by their sabbath rules.

Given the Pharisees' earlier silence, it should not surprise us that they reject this second opportunity. Particularly noteworthy is the force with which they reject it. "They went out and immediately held counsel with the Herodians against him how to destroy him." The Herodians, followers of Herod, ruled for Rome in northern Palestine, including Galilee. Normally, an orthodox Pharisee would have nothing to do with them. But their need to save face and preserve standing among men is so strong that it blinds them to their growing hypocrisy.

This story ends on a sober note. For though new consciousness can bring healing, it can also threaten others so that unconscious shadow problems become amplified. If we are not moving forward in life in a creative, healing way, then all too likely we will be pulled in the other direction to resist new spiritual consciousness, like the Pharisees. We are less and less able to live up to our own ideals, because we cannot see ourselves and life as God intended.

The real sign of the sabbath, of the synagogue, and of all religious life is healing. But those, like the Pharisees, who claim to follow a religious life may not follow it truly or honestly. Healing involves more than the discernment of spirits. It involves a consciousness that focuses on us as individuals and our individual relationship with God. Without this openness, there often cannot be healing. As we review the healing stories, we will see further how important this spiritual principle is to Jesus' healing work.

As usual with the healing stories in Mark, Matthew and Luke have their own modified versions (see note 5 for this chapter). In this case, John also contains a passage that comments on these issues.

"He who speaks on his own authority seeks his own glory; but he who seeks the glory of him who sent him is true, and in him there is no falsehood. Did not Moses give you the law? Yet none of you keeps the law. Why do you seek to kill me?" The people answered, "You have a demon! Who is seeking to kill you?" Jesus answered them, "I did one deed, and you all marvel at it. Moses gave you circumcision (not that it is from Moses, but from the fathers), and you circumcise a man upon the sabbath. If on the sabbath a man receives circumcision, so that the law of Moses may not be broken, are you angry with me because on the sabbath I made a man's whole body well? Do not judge by appearances, but judge with right judgment" (Jn 7:18–24).

This dialogue takes place in the temple, another holy place Jesus visited. At issue here is the law, the sabbath, and healing. What is the most important part of this or any religion? Jesus indicates that in his ministry he seeks glory only for God. The people (especially the Pharisees and other Jewish leaders) seek glory for themselves. They speak on their own authority and not God's, even though they claim to speak for God. Jesus refers to the law of Moses and to the people's disobedience.

Jesus indicates that the people want to kill him. As in Mark, he perceives what is really going on within them. They deny it, claiming he has a demon. They do not want to look into their own psyches, a very dangerous choice in these circumstances. Jesus refers to a deed he did at which they all marveled. From the context, we assume this marvelous deed involved healing. For Jesus compares circumcision on the sabbath, so that the law of Moses may not be broken, with making a man's body well on the sabbath. He implies that healing should certainly be a part of the sabbath, whether it be in a synagogue or the temple. Finally, he tells his hearers not to judge by appearance, but with "right judgment." When people are saving face and trying to appear religious, no healing will occur. Healing is a sign of right spiritual judgment and the proper development of spiritual consciousness.

The gospel passages involving healing on the sabbath imply that Jesus is trying to bring a new emphasis to religion, a focus lacking in the earlier Hebrew religious traditions. For Jesus religion must include making bodies well, which involves the development of individual consciousness. Without these elements, those called by God to develop further in life will only remain ill. Jesus' form of religion heals; that of the Pharisees promotes unconsciousness and illness. Thus the man in the story from Mark carries not only the symptom of his own illness, but the symptom for the illness of the Pharisees as well.

The relationship between healing and religion is also very important to Luke. In all of the healing stories he records that are not found in any of the other gospels, it is a primary concern. One of these stories, the healing of the ten lepers, we reviewed in Chapter 4.[13] We saw that it was the Samaritan, not the more traditional Jews, who responded most fully to God's healing. Another of the stories concerns the healing of the woman with the spirit of infirmity.

> Now he was teaching in one of the synagogues on the sabbath. And there was a woman who had had a spirit of infirmity for eighteen years; she was bent over and could not fully straighten herself. And when Jesus saw her, he called her and said to her, "Woman, you are freed from your infirmity." And he laid his hands upon her, and immediately she was made straight, and she praised God. But the ruler of the synagogue, indignant because Jesus had healed on the sabbath, said to the people, "There are six days on which work ought to be done; come on those days to be healed, and not on the sabbath day." Then the Lord answered him, "You hypocrites! Does not each of you on the sabbath untie his ox or his ass from the manger, and lead it away to water it? And ought not this woman, a daughter of Abraham whom Satan bound for eighteen years, be loosed from this bond on the sabbath day?" As he said this, all his adversaries were put to shame; and all the people rejoiced at all the glorious things that were done by him (Lk 13:10–17).

This story has many parallels to the healing of the man with the withered hand, but here the whole body of the person is "withered." The healing allows the woman to stand "straight" before God after carrying a great burden for many years. The story tells us that she has been bound by Satan. Hers was a spiritual problem as well as a physical one. Once again, the setting is the synagogue on the sabbath, the classic setting for comparison of the religious approach of Jesus to that of the Pharisees.

For eighteen years the woman endured her infirmity, even in the synagogue. As soon as Jesus lays hands on her she is healed. The contrast is startling. As in the stories we have just discussed, the religious authorities object rather than celebrate. The synagogue official, admonishing the people for coming to the synagogue on the sabbath to be healed and telling them to come on the other six days of the week, hides behind his religious legalism and dogmatism. He missed the opportunity to expand his own spiritual horizons to include healing like that which Jesus brings to this woman. Jesus does not let him off the hook. He responds quickly to confront him with his lack of consciousness. The question is not that of working on the sabbath at all. For no good Jew would hesitate to care for his animals on the sabbath. All the more so should this be true for human beings.

In this story, like others that raise the questions of religion and healing, we see an ill person with the right attitude for healing, someone ready for the proper shamanistic mediation. In this woman's case, her life is straightened out both physically and spiritually. She is free from the clutches of Satan because through Jesus she is freed from the unconscious darkness or shadow which lies within the chief official of the synagogue. In the healing process we see Jesus attempting to make such things conscious to those present. This is essential both for the healing of the woman and for the proper spiritual development of the synagogue leader.

In the last verse Luke tells us that all Jesus' adversaries were put to shame, and all the people rejoiced in the glorious things he was doing. It would certainly be marvelous to think this was the case, but it would not be in keeping with the other gospel records, especially those of Mark and John we have already reviewed. This verse would have to be seen as fitting Luke's own purposes at this point in his narrative. If this were actually the case, then it would seem that both Mark and John would have also indicated this to us.

Nor is this part of the story in keeping with human nature. Certainly the ruler of the synagogue was embarrassed. When human beings are faced with their own unconsciousness, they become defensive and their shadow sides are constellated as we saw in the story of the man with the withered hand. The status quo—especially the religious status quo—is not quickly changed or transformed. It does not easily lose its power and authority. Thus, it is not very likely that there was a dramatic change in the people who witnessed the event. There was certainly food for thought and wonder, but not wholesale collective change.

This is borne out later in the gospels when the Jewish leaders plot to do away with Jesus and his threat to their authority. They succeed in rousing the multitude against him while he is before Pilate. The development of a new consciousness that must come with spiritual healing is very individual and very fragile, especially when up against the collective thinking of the day.

Luke tells one other story, not found in the other gospels, that echoes the theme of this chapter. It is the healing of the man with dropsy.

> One sabbath when he went to dine at the house of a ruler who belonged to the Pharisees, they were watching him. And behold, there was a man before him who had dropsy. And Jesus spoke to the lawyers and Pharisees, saying, "Is it lawful to heal on the sabbath, or not?" But they were silent. Then he took him and healed him, and let him go. And he said to them, "Which of you, having a son or an ox that has fallen into a well, will not immediately pull him out on a sabbath day?" And they could not reply to this (Lk 14:1–6).

Once more we see parallels to other healing stories, especially the story of the man with the withered hand. Again it is the sabbath. This time the setting is the house of a ruler who belonged to the Pharisees. Luke notes that they were watching Jesus—trying to trip him up, perhaps. There is no sense of openness or genuine interest. Luke then tells us of the man with dropsy. Jesus stands between this man's need for healing and the watchful eye of the lawyers and Pharisees. He asks a question. "Is it lawful to heal on the sabbath, or not?" Should there not be an important place for healing? How does their religious law aid or hinder this? The Pharisees are again silent: they stay caught in their negativity and judge Jesus accordingly.

Jesus turns to the man with dropsy. The man is healed and Luke tells us that Jesus "let him go." Like the woman with the infirmity, he is freed from a spiritual condition, an unconscious negative attitude that kept him from being healed. As in the previous story, Jesus seeks to illuminate the absurdity of objections to healing on the sabbath and healing as part of the spiritual life. He challenges their basic fearful religious stance.

The Pharisees could not reply. They held both social and religious prestige and saw themselves in direct contact with God. Why give all this up and seek a new stance so that some sick people might be made well? Would it not be easier to discredit this man, and if necessary do away with him? It is profoundly ironic that men so concerned with religion were the most resistant to the healing Jesus offered.

These stories emphasize the difference between Jesus and the religious attitudes of his day. Jesus' healing is contrasted with the side of human nature that resists the deepest manifestations of the presence of God. Other stories develop this theme, emphasizing what qualities must emerge for us to be healed and to become agents of healing. We turn to these stories now.

NOTES

[1] For an example see Douglas Webster, "What Is Spiritual Healing?" pp. 6–7.

[2] Based on a study by Pelletier of seven "miracle" cancer cures. Other factors mentioned included change in diet, taking up some physical activity, revising personal and business lives to meet personal needs, and becoming involved with others in some form of outreach.

[3] Mk 5:25–34; discussed in Chapter 8.

[4] See Chapter 3.

[5] Parallels found in Mt 12:9–14 and Lk 6:6–11.

[6] Mk 2:23–27.

[7] See Mt 23 and Lk 11:37–12:3.

[8] Compare the far more spontaneous attitude to life of a shaman such as John Fire Lame Deer. See John Fire Lame Deer and Richard Erdoes, *Lame Deer, Seeker of Visions.*

[9] Mt 11:18–19 and Lk 7:33–34.

[10] Marie-Louise von Franz and James Hillman, *Jung's Typology.* John A. Sanford, *Evil: The Shadow Side of Reality,* Chapter 1. C.G. Jung, *Psychological Types,* CW, Vol. 6.

[11] C.G. Jung, *Memories, Dreams, Reflections,* pp. 247–48.

[12] James Lynch, *The Broken Heart.*

[13] Lk 17:11–19.

Chapter 6
Healing and Consciousness

T he condition Jesus healed most frequently was blindness. In the gospels blind people have sight restored and, more importantly, develop a special spiritual sight. Jesus was very adept at giving others a higher level of awareness. He perceived when people were being honest about their deeper motives and helped them become aware of deeper aspects of their personality. When they were healed, they could often "see" more—both within and around themselves.

There are three major accounts of the healing of the blind in the gospels, and many general references to Jesus' healing that usually include the blind. We have already discussed the healing of the blind man at Bethsaida.[1] We noted that in restoring his sight Jesus proposed a different relationship with his home village. Jesus suggests that he must now see things for himself and not as the villagers see them. If he remains in the village, he will not see life as he was meant to see it, will not reach the level of consciousness of which he is capable.

We also noted that Jesus must *touch* the man twice to heal him. We saw that Matthew and Luke left out this incident because it did not fit their portrayal of Jesus. Nevertheless, the development of this story is important to an understanding of healing, because it shows healing as a *process*. This fits with what we know about shamanistic healing and the development of human consciousness. They reflect an ongoing process, with occasional ecstatic breakthroughs. They must include encounters with the darker aspects of ourselves and of life, as seen in Jesus' temptations in the wilderness. The two steps of healing can be seen as the improvement of this man's sight and the development of his consciousness.

When the man first begins to "see" he says, "I see men; but they look like trees, walking." The image is a good one for the development of human consciousness. The man is beginning to see men, but not clearly. By comparison, Jesus sees people very clearly. He reads their hearts, their hidden potential, and their hidden malice. At first this man sees nothing. Then he sees men as trees walking. He perceives them as living and somewhat distinct, but not in human form. An undeveloped consciousness, one influenced by a group standpoint, perceives only the forest, not the trees. This was probably the attitude of the village the man came from. "Conform to our standards or you will not be seen. You cannot be an individual here." Separated from the village, he can now sense the trees as separate from the forest. When Jesus takes him off alone, it may be the first time that someone is relating to him as an individual.

When Jesus touches the man the second time, he sees everything clearly. We sense that he not only sees, but sees with spiritual clarity. He sees things for himself and not as the ethos of the village might dictate. Jesus' instruction not to return to the village implies just how fragile the man's inner development is. If he returned to the village, he could lose his new consciousness and be blinded again.

The development of this man's sight suggests a related instance in Mark's gospel, the story of the blind beggar Bartimaeus.

> And they came to Jericho; and as he was leaving Jericho with his disciples and a great multitude, Bartimaeus, a blind beggar, the son of Timaeus, was sitting by the roadside. And when he heard that it was Jesus of Nazareth, he began to cry out and say, "Jesus, Son of David, have mercy on me!" And many rebuked him, telling him to be silent; but he cried out all the more, "Son of David, have mercy on me!" And Jesus stopped and said, "Call him." And they called the blind man, saying to him, "Take heart; rise, he is calling you." And throwing off his mantle he sprang up and came to Jesus. And Jesus said to him, "What do you want me to do for you?" And the blind man said to him, "Master, let me receive my sight." And Jesus said to him, "Go your way; your faith has made you well." And immediately he received his sight and followed him on the way (Mk 10:46–52).[2]

It is very likely that Bartimaeus was reduced to beggar status after he became blind. Society judged his blindness as showing disfavor in the eyes of God and ostracized him. Sitting by the roadside, he hears a great multitude and learns that Jesus of Nazareth is coming. He begins to cry out, "Jesus, Son of David, have mercy on me!" For a beggar this is remarkable. By crying out, Bartimaeus boldly challenged the society that had reduced him to his lowly status. Many in the crowd rebuked him, telling him to be silent. But he had had enough of their rejection and cried out all the more, "Jesus, Son of David, have mercy on me!"

In this call Bartimaeus links two important terms—"Son of David" and "mercy." In the context of the gospels and of the Israelite religion, a son of David lived in proper relationship with God in the spirit of David.[3] One living thus would show mercy to others. Bartimaeus had not experienced much mercy—only rejection. Somehow he sensed that Jesus was different, not like others he had known who claimed to be carrying on the heritage of David.

Therefore, Bartimaeus challenges Jesus boldly, saying: "Son of David show mercy, which I have yet to be shown; will you have mercy on me? If so, then you are a true son of David." Seeing this man's nerve and determination, Jesus recognizes a candidate for healing and discipleship, so he calls the man over. Bartimaeus' persistence has paid off.

Those who carry Jesus' message say an interesting thing to Bartimaeus: "Take heart." We discussed the word "heart" in connection with the hardness of heart of the Pharisees. We see in Bartimaeus the opposite quality, for he has heart. This man, despised, rejected, seen as being in disfavor with God, possesses the most important quality of the spiritual life. It shows in his bold call to Jesus and his sense of the importance of mercy. Bartimaeus speaks with great emotion, a quality missing from the Pharisees and abundant in Jesus.

When he hears that Jesus is calling him, Bartimaeus throws off his mantle. He has found a kindred spirit. He no longer has to go around cloaked in the mantle of his society and his religion. He can be his true self and not the beggar. When Bartimaeus and Jesus meet there is real excitement; both seem glad to have found each other. Jesus makes an open offer: "What do you want me to do for you?" Bartimaeus replies, "Let me receive my sight." It is important to recognize what this request encompasses. To be healed of his sight means that Bartimaeus would also cease to be a beggar, rebuked and ridiculed; he could be a human being again. Like Solomon in the Old Testament, he requests a gift that would affect his whole being.

Understanding the depth of the request, Jesus says simply, "Go your way; your faith has made you well." He takes no credit for the healing; Bartimaeus' faith has made him well. Bartimaeus has come into touch with something in himself that lets him go forward into life in a new way.

As Jesus approached him, Bartimaeus was filled with spiritual insight. This insight had probably been bubbling around him for some time, but now he gives it open expression. Bartimaeus sees—in the deepest sense. The faith that burst forth in him leads to the healing of his physical blindness. The blindness can be seen as a wilderness experience, and not a

punishment for wrongdoing. It was a call to a deeper religious consciousness. The Pharisees' interpretation of his illness made him a beggar, but the
rejection and isolation that came with it stirred a life energy deep within.
His treatment at the hands of society showed him both the hypocrisy of his
religion and its true nature.

As this healing story ends, Bartimaeus sees clearly, physically and
spiritually. But it is especially because of his spiritual sight that we are told
that he followed Jesus on the way. The Greek word *hodos,* here translated
as "way," was a euphemism for early Christians, who called their life "the
way." Bartimaeus discovered his own way, the living nature of his religion,
a faith that can transform both body and soul.

The third story, from John, involves a man who was born blind. It is
the longest healing story in the gospels, and it develops many of the themes
in the shorter Markan accounts.

> As he passed by, he saw a man blind from his birth. And his
> disciples asked him, "Rabbi, who sinned, this man or his parents,
> that he was born blind?" Jesus answered, "It was not that this
> man sinned, or his parents, but that the works of God might be
> made manifest in him. We must work the works of him who sent
> me, while it is day; night comes, when no one can work. As long
> as I am in the world, I am the light of the world." As he said this,
> he spat on the ground and made clay of the spittle and anointed
> the man's eyes with the clay, saying to him, "Go, wash in the
> pool of Siloam" (which means Sent). So he went and washed and
> came back seeing. The neighbors and those who had seen him
> before as a beggar said, "Is not this the man who used to sit and
> beg?" Some said, "It is he"; others said, "No, but he is like him."
> He said, "I am the man." They said to him, "Then how were
> your eyes opened?" He answered, "The man called Jesus made
> clay and anointed my eyes and said to me, 'Go to Siloam and
> wash'; so I went and washed and received my sight." They said
> to him, "Where is he?" He said, "I do not know."
>
> They brought to the Pharisees the man who had formerly
> been blind. Now it was a sabbath day when Jesus made the clay
> and opened his eyes. The Pharisees again asked him how he had
> received his sight. And he said to them, "He put clay on my eyes,
> and I washed, and I see." Some of the Pharisees said, "This man
> is not from God, for he does not keep the sabbath." But others

said, "How can a man who is a sinner do such signs?" There was a division among them. So they again said to the blind man, "What do you say about him, since he has opened your eyes?" He said, "He is a prophet."

The Jews did not believe that he had been blind and had received his sight, until they called the parents of the man who had received his sight and asked them, "Is this your son, who you say was born blind? How then does he now see?" His parents answered, "We know that this is our son, and that he was born blind; but how he now sees we do not know, nor do we know who opened his eyes. Ask him; he is of age; he will speak for himself." His parents said this because they feared the Jews, for the Jews had already agreed that if any one should confess him to be Christ, he was to be put out of the synagogue. Therefore, his parents said, "He is of age, ask him."

For the second time they called the man who had been blind, and said to him, "Give God the praise; we know that this man is a sinner." He answered, "Whether he is a sinner, I do not know; one thing I know, that though I was blind, now I see." They said to him, "What did he do to you? How did he open your eyes?" He answered them, "I have told you already, and you would not listen. Why do you want to hear it again? Do you too want to become his disciples?" And they reviled him, saying, "You are his disciple, but we are the disciples of Moses. We know that God has spoken to Moses, but as for this man, we do not know where he comes from." The man answered, "Why, this is a marvel! You do not know where he comes from, yet he opened my eyes. We know that God does not listen to sinners, but if any one is a worshiper of God and does his will, God listens to him. Never since the world began has it been heard that any one opened the eyes of a man born blind. If this man were not from God, he could do nothing." They answered him, "You were born in utter sin, and would you teach us?" And they cast him out.

Jesus heard that they had cast him out, and having found him he said, "Do you believe in the Son of man?" He answered, "And who is he, sir, that I may believe in him?" Jesus said to him, "You have seen him, and it is he who speaks to you." He said, "Lord, I believe"; and he worshiped him. Jesus said, "For judgment I came into this world, that those who do not see may see,

and that those who see may become blind." Some of the Pharisees near him heard this, and they said to him, "Are we also
blind?" Jesus said to them, "If you were blind, you would have
no guilt; but now that you say, 'We see,' your guilt remains"
(Jn 9).

This man has been blind from birth. Like Bartimaeus, he is a beggar
who sits by the side of the road. Jesus' disciples ask of him, "Who sinned,
this man or his parents, that he was born blind?" This question reflects the
attitude of the time and culture toward illness: it is the result of sin. Jesus
introduces an entirely different notion. Illness is *not* necessarily the result of
sin. Instead, it can be a unique, though obviously paradoxical, way for the
will of God to manifest itself. God's primary intent is healing, and healing
takes place when there is a development of consciousness. Illness pushes
the afflicted person toward higher consciousness and spiritual awareness.
The sick individual is not cut off from God, but moved to a place where he
might better see God's purposes. The plagues and illnesses surrounding the
escape from Egypt and the wilderness experience of the Old Testament,
for example, can be seen not as punishments but as events meant to spur
people into fuller participation in God's design.

Jesus surprises the disciples with his response, and presents them with
an extraordinary mandate. "*We* must work the works of him who sent
me." He goes on to say that they must do this while it is day, that when
night comes no one can work. In this context, "day" refers to the light of
consciousness. Where there is consciousness, healing can emerge. While
Jesus is in the world, he provides this light of consciousness. But soon he
will leave his disciples, and it will be up to them to bear this light. They
must become able to do this work. They must learn the purpose of illness
and how healing takes place.

At this point Jesus heals the man born blind. He does so like a
shaman—spitting on the ground, making clay of the spittle, and anointing
the man's eyes. Then he sends the man off to wash in the pool whose name
means "sent." He involves the man all along—in completing the instructions, journeying to the pool and washing; he returns able to see. He is a
changed man, but, as often happens when people change, the "neighbors"
do not recognize him. We recall the problem Jesus' neighbors had when he
returned to his home town as a very successful teacher and healer.[4] The
man born blind finds some acceptance. When he tells them that he is the
same man, they inquire how he was healed. When his neighbors ask where

Jesus is, the man replies that he does not know. The man has been cured, but his inner development is still continuing. He does not yet understand his transformation and, like the Geresene demonic, he can only relate the account of his healing.

Now the man is brought before the Pharisees. It was on the sabbath that Jesus healed him. The Pharisees take their turn questioning the man, an important event in his ongoing development—forcing him to look at his recent experience in light of the teaching of these religious leaders. He retells his story. However, as we have seen, the Pharisees are not honest. Some of them say about Jesus, "This man is not from God, for he does not keep the sabbath." John is probably more realistic in his portrayal of the Pharisees than the other three evangelists. He presents another group of Pharisees who are less quick to judge and more willing to consider the facts. So they say, "How can a man who is a sinner do such signs?" It is a good question, and it divides the Pharisees. So they turn to the man to see what he has to say about the man who healed him. He responds, "He is a prophet."

This is too much for any of the Pharisees to accept. Having a legitimate prophet in Israel would threaten their authority. Rather than accept the man's report concerning Jesus, they look for ways to undermine his testimony. They send for his parents, for they have convinced themselves that the man could not possibly have been born blind. The parents bear witness to the truth—this is indeed their son, and he was born blind. They do not know how it is that he sees, or who opened his eyes. They stay with the facts. They have no further experience, so they tell the Pharisees, "Ask him; he is of age; he will speak for himself." This is an important statement, especially from a psychological perspective. If a person's parents continue to speak for him, that individual never has a chance to develop on his own. The parents of this man will not try to speak for their son and fill in the gap. When we consider that the son was born with a handicap, we can easily imagine how his parents might have become accustomed to stepping into situations for him.

Quite likely, as the evangelist states, the parents deferred to their son out of fear of the Jews. This statement seems to be an editorial comment by the evangelist, however. The parents did not know how their son was healed or anything about the healer. After he was healed, the son could not tell anyone where his healer had gone. His parents can say no more, but they recognize that there has been more than just a physical change. Their son is not only legally old enough to speak for himself (for many children are and their parents still want to speak for them), but psychologically and spiritually able as well.

The Pharisees have no recourse but to talk again to the man, hoping to discredit Jesus in the process. If they had not been obsessed with doing so, they might not have bothered to speak to the man again. They say to him, "Give God the praise; we know that this man is a sinner." We notice how certain they are in this, how they press this certainty on the man. But he stays within his own experience. He responds, "Whether he is a sinner, I do not know (for isn't it only God who really knows this about others?); one thing I know, that though I was blind, now I see." His knowledge, his consciousness, are within the limits of his God-given experience. Once again the Pharisees ask the man how his eyes were opened. We begin to realize that he sees with more than just his eyes. He has come of age spiritually. In a style that Jesus used quite frequently, he asks the Pharisees, "I have told you already, and you would not listen. Why do you want to hear it again?" The man now sees through their hypocrisy. He has a new consciousness, grown out of his original encounter with Jesus. His realization is similar to the one that came to the man with the withered hand.[5] This man, however, assesses the Pharisees completely on his own and asks the questions. In the story of the man with the withered hand, Jesus asked the questions.

The man is no longer intimidated by the Pharisees. His healing experience has strengthened him, and he refuses to put up with their duplicity any longer. He gives them a chance to realize what they are really doing in not accepting the facts of his experience. The Pharisees, however, do not want to believe that someone acting outside their belief system can do such things. They are not asking about his experience to learn, but out of malice so as to discredit it. It is most important that they answer in their hearts the man's question, "Why do you want to hear it again?" His second question is even more cutting: "Do you too want to become his disciples?" Of course not—they are trying to discredit him. But the only honest reason for continuing to question this man about his healing experience would be to learn about healing. Clearly, Jesus can perform a special kind of spiritual transformation that the Pharisees cannot.

Naturally the Pharisees do not like this man's questions. Any inquiry that touches on the unconscious, especially one that threatens the mask we like to present to the world, is likely to get us riled up. Since this man's questions get to the heart of the Pharisees' unconsciousness, they make them irritated and defensive. So they reviled the man, saying, "You are his disciple, but we are disciples of Moses. We know that God has spoken to Moses, but as for this man, we do not know where he comes from." The man was not a disciple of Jesus, not yet anyway. He had been healed by him, but then had lost contact with him. As we shall see in a moment, his encounter with the Pharisees has made him a prime candidate for disciple-ship. The Pharisees try to place the man in an inferior position; they have become name-droppers. If you are a devout Hebrew, the biggest name you can use is that of Moses, for Moses was closer to God than anyone, and of course they were disciples of Moses.

The man is not intimidated. Now that he has spoken out so well from his heart, he continues to do so with penetrating insight. He says to them, "Why, this is a marvel! You do not know where he comes from, and yet he opened my eyes. We know that God does not listen to sinners, but if any one is a worshiper of God and does his will, God listens to him. Never since the world began has it been heard that any one opened the eyes of a man born blind. If this man were not from God, he could do nothing." Again we hear clever sarcasm combined with extraordinary perception. These men who claim to be disciples of Moses also claim they do not know where Jesus comes from. They had hoped to dismiss the man as a disciple of Jesus. In their eyes, to be associated with Jesus meant one was a long way from being associated with Moses. The formerly blind man sees right through this sham. How could they not know where Jesus came from if he heals? Doesn't healing come from God? Where else could it come from? This healing is an extraordinary new thing, just as Moses offered the people an extraordinary experience of God. If a person was a sinner, and thus not truly in contact with God, he could not do such marvelous things. Moses fulfilled God's will, taught the proper worship of God, and God was there with Moses during his life's work. This man is doing God's work, and therefore he too must be doing God's will. Are you really disciples of Moses if you do not see this?

This man's inspired speech puts an end to the meeting with the Phari-sees. After such a statement they can do nothing but face their hypocrisy, or give up their own attempts to influence him. Since they were not able to grow spiritually, they revert to their original contempt for this man and cast him out. He was born blind; therefore, he was and remains a sinner. They will have nothing to do with him. "Would you teach us?" The Phari-sees have missed how much God has come to reside in this man.

The man's last encounter with Jesus verifies his spiritual transforma-tion. Hearing what has happened, Jesus asks him an interesting question:

"Do you believe in the Son of man?" The former blind man responds as if he does not know this Son of man. "And who is he, sir, that I may believe in him?" Jesus said to him, "You have seen him, and it is he who speaks to you." This response can be viewed in two ways. Traditionally, most people have assumed Jesus is referring to himself. The man had seen Jesus when he first healed him, and now of course Jesus is speaking to him. However, there is another way of looking at this final encounter.

We have already noted that the final author of the gospel of John probably influenced it in spots, as when the Pharisees interviewed the man's parents. The editorializing comes into play here, but not enough to hide the story's original intent. Jesus tells the man that he has already seen the Son of man. We can ask: When was this? Was it back when he was first healed? No. When the man first encountered Jesus, he could not see. After anointing him with clay, Jesus sent the man off to wash in the pool of Siloam, where he gains his sight. However, Jesus was no longer with him. Thus, when his neighbors ask him where Jesus is, he does not know, because he has not seen Jesus after regaining his sight. So when did he see the Son of man? He saw the Son of man when he spoke before the Pharisees. When he "saw" clearly enough to speak to the Pharisees, he was seeing the Son of man. And it was here that the Son of man began to speak to him.

This was a crucial point in the man's religious development; he learned to hear the voice of God within. This is an important theme elsewhere in John's gospel. Jesus will leave the disciples to return to the Father. They will have to rely on the Spirit, the inner voice of God. This man already hears that voice. The remarkable development that has taken place in him would be set back if he had to rely on an external figure to articulate his new insight. While he certainly needed Jesus' intervention to be healed and to begin his spiritual development, now it is most important that he continue to recognize, listen to, and worship the inner voice of God. Thus the Son of man can be seen in the life of Jesus, but it also can be seen within. Thus Jesus spoke of the Son of man in the third person as if it was a figure he also saw within himself.[6]

The belief of the man Jesus healed is not focused only on Jesus, but on the divine, inspiring voice within. His faith is based on a personal experience of profound transformation in both body and soul. This man stayed in living contact with the inner voice that spoke to him and that Jesus made it possible for him to discover. Such worship stands in opposition to the practices of the Pharisees, who no longer hear the divine voice that spoke to Moses—either in the man born blind, in Jesus, or in themselves.

The final three verses of the passage summarize Jesus' evaluation of the Pharisees. We hear that he has come into the world for a unique judgment: "that those who do not see may see, and that those who see may become blind." The first part of this judgment applies to those like the blind man, who saw neither physically nor spiritually, but who came to see very clearly in both ways. But what about the second group? In the story, some of the Pharisees hear this statement and sense that it applies to them. They ask, "Are we also blind?" Jesus makes an important response. If it were simply a question of their being blind, there would be no guilt, and no sin, as with the man born blind. He had no sin because neither he nor his parents professed to see or understand why he was ill. The Pharisees, on the other hand, claimed that he was indeed a sinner. They professed to understand how God judged his world and his people. But it is clear that they did not. It was they who had sinned, and theirs was the greatest of all sins, religious hypocrisy. The blind man and his family suffered because of their sin. Not to see was one thing, but to claim to see and yet *not* see was a great sin. Because they were so convinced that they did see, the Pharisees could not accept Jesus or hear what the man born blind was telling them.

The healing of this man shows that illness does not necessarily imply sin. It can be seen as a call from God to greater spiritual consciousness. Shamans, we recall, usually receive their call through an initiatory illness. The story also makes it clear that those who seem healthy in a sense, like the Pharisees, may suffer from a spiritual illness—one that in turn contributes to the suffering of others. Here we find real sin. However, some cases in the gospels do indicate a real relationship between sin and physical illness. In such cases the problem of sin must be recognized before true healing can begin.

NOTES

[1] Mk 8:22–26; see Chapters 2 and 4.

[2] Parallels found in Mt 20:29–34 and Lk 18:35–43.

[3] For example, both Matthew and Luke (Mt 1:1–16 and Lk 3:23–38) present genealogies which appear to trace Jesus' biological lineage to David. However, they do so by tracing Joseph's ancestry, not Mary's. The genealogies thus emphasize that Jesus carries the *spiritual* heritage of David, not his historical ancestry.

[4] See Chapter 2, the discussion about Mk 6:1–6a.

[5] Mk 3:1–6; see Chapter 5.

[6] See Frederick H. Borsch, *The Son of Man in Myth and History,* for an excellent review of this Christological designation and its roots in Hebrew tradition.

Chapter 7
Healing and Sin

O ne of the most dramatic stories in the gospels is the healing of a paralytic whose friends lower him through the roof to Jesus. The story contains many significant lessons—the importance of a highly developed consciousness, of faith, and forgiveness. Mark tells the story this way.

> And when he returned to Capernaum after some days, it was reported that he was at home. And many were gathered to gether, so that there was no longer room for them, not even about the door; and he was preaching the word to them. And they came, bringing to him a paralytic carried by four men. And when they could not get near him because of the crowd, they removed the roof above him; and when they had made an open ing, they let down the pallet on which the paralytic lay. And when Jesus saw their faith, he said to the paralytic, "My son, your sins are forgiven." Now some of the scribes were sitting there, questioning in their hearts, "Why does this man speak thus? It is blasphemy! Who can forgive sins but God alone?" And immediately Jesus, perceiving in his spirit that they thus ques tioned within themselves, said to them, "Why do you question thus in your hearts? Which is easier, to say to the paralytic, 'Your sins are forgiven,' or to say, 'Rise, take up your pallet and walk'? But that you may know that the Son of man has authority on earth to forgive sins"—he said to the paralytic—"I say to you, rise, take up your pallet and go home." And he rose, and immedi ately took up the pallet and went out before them all; so that they were all amazed and glorified God, saying, "We never saw anything like this" (Mk 2:1–12).[1]

The setting helps us understand the drama. Jesus was "at home" in Capernaum. Either he had a home there, or was staying with someone else. The place is packed with people listening to him. Suddenly, in comes a group of four men carrying the paralytic. They must have been very determined, not to be discouraged by so large a crowd. They take the man up to the roof, make an opening, and lower him down to Jesus—an extraordinary act of friendship and great faith.

How would we react if this happened in our house? Jesus' response is remarkable. Instead of becoming angry at what was happening on the roof, he perceives right away what motivates the men. That motivation is what matters most, for Jesus sees men's hearts. Early in his gospel, John relates that when Jesus first went to Jerusalem, many believed in his signs, but he did not trust them, because "he knew all men and needed no one to bear witness of man; for he himself knew what was in man" (Jn 2:25). In evaluating other people, Jesus was less concerned with outward actions than with the personalities within. Many people—like the Pharisees—appeared proper enough on the outside but were inwardly confused and self-righteous. Others—the sick and so-called tax collectors and sinners—looked unacceptable and unworthy of any blessing from God, yet had great spiritual potential within. In this story, however destructive the action of the men carrying the paralytic, Jesus saw it as an act of faith coming from their depths.

Jesus perceived people in terms of their relation to the unconscious, as the language of depth psychology would put it. He saw their potential for a richer, fuller life. He also perceived when people were dishonest with themselves, when they lived for appearances and hid their true God-given personalities. This extraordinary awareness of people's psyches is what allowed Jesus to heal. Our story shows that he perceived not only the influence of clean and unclean spirits, but also what went on in their individual lives.

Having grasped the motivation of the paralytic's friends, Jesus turns to the paralytic himself. Without preamble, he says, "My son, your sins are forgiven." This statement is unusual. Most of the healing stories contain no mention of sin. In this man, however, Jesus perceives something to indicate that the paralysis results from sin. Jesus first addresses the man as "My son," the Greek *teknon* implying that he sees the man as his spiritual child and takes a strong personal interest in him. Jesus' words of forgiveness here are the most endearing and gentle of any he makes anywhere in the gospels.

The perception of sin as underlying the man's paralysis raises the issue of guilt. People dominated by guilt usually feel a deep personal unworthiness. Sometimes no specific act accounts for this feeling. Many who grew up in rigid environments, religious or not, live with guilt. The burden can become so strong that their lives become paralyzed—if not physically like this man, then spiritually and psychologically. Such people cannot live authentically on their own. They depend too much on the views of others and on the social and religious conventions of the day.

Some degree of guilt can obviously be necessary and healthy. But in our culture there is usually too much of it. Many patients in therapy, burdened by guilt and external demands, lack the zest and enthusiasm to live life fully. As children, they reacted to protect themselves from authority figures. Much of their natural emotional energy became bottled up. The paralytic seems to have been such a man. Fortunately, his friends cared deeply for him and possessed the energy to put him in contact with genuine healing. Jesus, likewise, realizes that the man will view him as a spiritual authority and probably feel frightened and embarrassed by what his friends have done. Most likely in the past he has not had good encounters with authority figures. With his first statement, Jesus wants to allay the man's fears. Not only does he take the man under his personal care, he addresses himself immediately to his sense of sin and guilt.

As so often happens in the healing stories, the Pharisees watch what Jesus is doing, waiting to judge and condemn him. They are "questioning in their hearts," but not outwardly. Their critical thoughts and judgments are the most destructive. Once again Jesus perceives this hidden malice and tries to bring it out in the open. He asks them, "Why do you question thus in your hearts?" All people have questions inside of them. They should not be left within, however, but brought out into the light of consciousness, where they can be honestly wrestled with. John tells us that Jesus was the light of the world (Jn 1:1–9).[2] The light of the world is the light of consciousness. Jesus' healing called for precisely such consciousness.

What the scribes question in their hearts is Jesus' reference to the forgiveness of sins. They find it audacious, even blasphemous. They believe—correctly—that God alone can forgive sins. They are not totally wrong, but partially so, and that is enough to create a deep misunderstanding. The difficulty is that they keep it inside rather than risk open dialogue with Jesus, even when he provides the opportunity.

Part of the trouble the scribes face in this story stems from their not hearing what Jesus said to the man. Instead, they heard what they *wanted* to hear: "My son, *I* forgive you your sins." They heard Jesus was claiming to be on a level with God, and that was blasphemy. A close reading of the gospels reveals that while Jesus indicates he has a very close relationship with God, he never claims to *be* God. He also invites others to experience the same intimacy with God. What Jesus actually told the paralytic was, "My son, your sins are forgiven"—a reminder that God's true nature is to forgive sins.

The forgiveness of sins is not new to Jesus and the New Testament. The Old Testament describes it as well. For example, God speaks through the prophet Isaiah: "I, I am he who blots out your transgressions for my own sake, and I will not remember your sins" (Is 43:25). Jesus reminds the paralytic of this aspect of God when he says, "Your sins are forgiven." The words of Psalm 103 attribute both healing and the forgiveness of sins to God's nature: "Bless the Lord, O my soul, and forget not all his benefits, who forgives all your iniquity, who heals all your diseases" (Ps 103:2–3). Jesus confronts the scribes with this aspect of their common religious heritage when he asks, "Which is easier, to say to the paralytic, 'Your sins are forgiven,' or to say, 'Rise, take up your pallet and walk'?"

New Testament scholars point out that the Greek word for sin, *harmartia,* is an old archery term meaning "to miss the mark." As we attempt to go the spiritual way and fulfill God's will, it is natural to miss the mark. God is interested in calling our attention to this and sometimes he does so through illness. But God intends us to go forward, not to dwell on the past and be condemned for it. As in archery, we are asked to reset ourselves and try again. God is interested in a new future. Again it is Isaiah who expresses this sense of sin as he speaks the words of God. "Remember not the former things, nor consider the things of old. Behold, I am doing a new thing; now it springs forth, do you not perceive it?" (Is 43:18–19a).[3]

Jesus knows the Israelite tradition and its healing intentions better than the Pharisaic scribes. Whatever this man's sin, the scribes have more deeply missed the mark. In this story the differences between Jesus and the Pharisees center on questions of forgiveness, judgment, and blasphemy. Though the Pharisees recognize the theological point that only God can forgive sins, they have obviously lost contact with the capacity to mediate this kind of experience to others. This has happened because of their moralistic, judging attitude. They approach the sick in the gospels with this attitude and they use it to condemn Jesus.

While the Pharisees realize that only God can forgive sins, they have forgotten that only God can judge. Blinded by their sin of judging in the name of God, they are not open to the things Jesus is doing and do not see them clearly. Ironically, Jesus can heal those whom the Pharisees have written off. Many of the gospel stories address this balance between forgiveness and judgment. In one passage in Luke a woman comes to Jesus

and anoints his feet with oil. She has been a notorious sinner in the eyes of
the Pharisees. At the end of the story Jesus offers her the same kind of
reminder he offers to the paralytic: "Your sins are forgiven" (Lk 7:36–50).
Other passages wrestle with similar issues.[4] They are summed up in this
teaching of Jesus: "Judge not, and you will not be judged; condemn not,
and you will not be condemned; forgive, and you will be forgiven"
(Lk 6:37).

The Pharisees will be judged by God for the very sin they accuse Jesus
of committing—blasphemy. They will seek the death sentence for Jesus,
accusing him of their sin. They misperceive what Jesus said about forgiveness. They do not comprehend what God would do in the lives of so many
who come to Jesus. They unconsciously identify their judgments of others
with the judgment of God. They are playing God with the lives of other
people. Their sin is blasphemy, an unconscious sin they refuse to recognize.
The unconscious sin gets projected onto others, and others pay the price.
Jesus sought a proper balance in such matters. In the gospel of John he tells
his disciples that this will be the function of the counselor—the Holy
Spirit—who will come when he is gone. "And when he comes he will
convince the world concerning righteousness and judgment" (Jn 16:8).

After almost two thousand years of Christianity, not much of the
world, especially the Christian world, has been convinced by the counselor
about these things. The gospels indicate that the proper relationship between forgiveness and judgment leads to a productive healing ministry.
The absence of such a ministry in Christian life today indicates that much
spiritual work remains to be done. A good example of the Pharisaic problems that surface within Christianity occurred during the reformation.
When Luther broke from the Church of Rome, the pope openly de-
nounced him as Satan, and Luther responded in kind. Neither one embod-
ied Satan, of course, but their language shows the degree of spiritual inflation from which both men suffered. Blatantly to describe another person
as Satan implies that one has definitive knowledge of God. The absolute
discernment of good and evil is a spiritual judgment of the highest order.
Both men were caught by the unconscious darkness within their own souls.
They had not wrestled with it as Jesus had done in the wilderness. Rather
than face their own need for power and be able to more objectively
evaluate the other, they projected their own psychological shadows onto
each other.

Jesus challenged the Pharisees to face their spiritual paralysis, their
inability to forgive and heal and thus perceive God's movement in life.

Jesus threatened their false sense of spiritual authority. His challenge to the Pharisees here recalls his challenge at the end of the story of the healing of the man born blind. There we saw Jesus confront them with their sin, a sin born out of the fact that they claimed to see, and obviously they do not. When Jesus speaks to them, he raises important issues of religion and life. They are obviously deficient in this respect, because they do not see the potential for healing. It becomes clear that in many ways they are responsible for this man's paralysis.

We have seen that this man probably carried a great burden of guilt and that the guilt paralyzed him. He would have received his sense of guilt directly or indirectly from the Pharisees and their approach to the Israelite tradition. Elsewhere in the gospels Jesus specifically states his case: "They [the Pharisees] bind heavy burdens, hard to bear, and lay them on men's shoulders; but they themselves will not move them with their finger" (Mt 23:4).[5] The paralytic is a living example. Religion has become sick. Jesus' teaching and healing ministries point out this frightening and important truth. The worst enemies of religion usually lie within religion itself. A subtle rigidity takes over that blocks the flow of healing.

It would be very easy to say that the problem in the gospels was one of Jesus' own time, that it stemmed from the branch of Judaism known as Pharisaism. However, this is not the case. Theologically, Jesus was probably as close to the point of view of the Pharisees as to any other Hebrew sect. The Pharisees should be viewed as an attitude toward religion, rather than a specific theology. Theirs is an all-too-human attitude, equally prevalent today. It is legalistic, moralistic, and lacks real feeling. It can be found in any religion and any branch of Christianity. Many in psychotherapy suffer from the spiritual environment in which they labor. They may not even be involved in the church but carry within themselves a paralyzing religious outlook they picked up in childhood.

Such spiritual discomfort is usually not consciously inflicted, and pastoral care has every intention of alleviating its symptoms. But the reality is that in most cases nothing is changed, and in many cases the situation is actually made worse. Pharisaism at its best establishes a ministry of visitation and comforting of the sick, and at its worst deepens the burden of personal doubt and unworthiness that can accompany any illness. Jesus makes it clear that a fully developed religion offers not just comfort, but healing. Healing, however, is not easily obtained. It requires a great deal of inner work and an honest confrontation with one's Pharisaic side.

Psychotherapeutic healing is greatly facilitated in certain individuals who live in church communities that nurture the healing process. These communities alleviate some of the emotional burdens of early life, give people assistance in discovering their unique value, and help fill them with a sense of the presence of God. Such community experience does not preclude individual psychotherapy and the development of personal consciousness, but it can help heal the soul. On the whole, however, when we talk about healing in the church today, we talk far more about untapped spiritual potential than about something Christians have realized. Just as the forgiveness of sins was an unrealized part of the religious tradition of the Pharisees, so healing is an unlived part of our religious heritage as Christians.

As the story ends, Jesus again turns to the paralytic. Like the man with the withered hand, this man has been present for Jesus' conversation with the Pharisees. For a while Jesus turns from the man's individual situation to the problem of the Pharisaic attitude. Now he turns back. Jesus asks the Pharisees, "Which is easier to say, to the paralytic, 'Your sins are forgiven,' or to say 'Rise, take up your pallet and walk'?" He then refers to the Son of man as having the authority to forgive sins. Again Jesus speaks in the third person, implying that the Son of man is an objective spiritual reality available to anyone. Part of the experience of the Son of man is a release from the burden of sin, much as it was an inspiring experience to the man born blind.

The forgiveness of sins is an inner experience, usually facilitated by outer circumstances. Likewise for healing. Jesus gives the paralytic the final push to discover his inner strength and go forward with new energy and purpose. "I say to you, rise, take up your pallet and go home." Here Jesus takes a very personal stand, opposite to that of the Pharisees. The man's life has been rooted in the voices of Pharisaism burdening him with guilt, taking away any true sense of self and purpose as seen through the eyes of God. Now he has worth and value. Jesus addresses him personally, and then challenges the Pharisees. In so doing, he is also challenging those same voices within this man. There has been an important dramatic buildup of Jesus' final instruction to this man, a very therapeutic one. The alternatives are these: The Pharisees say to you that you are a sinner, they burden you with unnecessary burdens, they have cut you off from God. I say to you, take up your pallet and get on with your life. Which is it going to be?

This is the crucial point. The time has come to act. The man must pick up his pallet; no one else can do it for him. If he had not tried, he would

remain bound by the burden of the Pharisees. In psychotherapy, the therapist can provide a healthy atmosphere and assist the process, but it is the
person himself who must act, must respond personally to the new opportunities the therapy affords. The paralytic, by picking up his pallet, acts with
a boldness previously seen only in his friends and in Jesus. He gained this
boldness from them, and he reached a new awareness of his predicament
from the conversation Jesus had with the Pharisees. He can begin to live in
a new way.

Learning to live with a new consciousness is important in most cases
of healing. This man, especially, had a strong sense of sin. He was sensitive
and guilt-ridden because of the Pharisees. His body was paralyzed and his
life was paralyzed. He could not act. It is doubtful whether this man had
really committed any truly terrible sin, even from the perspective of Phara-
saic teaching. However, from an inner perspective he was guilty of another
kind of sin, a sin of omission. He had not lived life fully enough. He had
become too afraid of life. This form of sin denies much of the God-given
life within. It is what Jesus meant by a sin against the spirit. It implies an
inherent distrust of the reality of God working through our lives.

In the gospels Jesus never condemns anyone the Pharisees condemn.
He is not concerned with sins of commission. These can always be re-
deemed. There are many examples: the woman who came to Jesus at the
Pharisee's house and anointed his feet with ointment;[6] the adulteress
whom the Pharisees tried to get Jesus to judge;[7] the prodigal son.[8] The
prodigal son lived boldly, and though he made mistakes along the way, he
embraced life and came to a deeper relationship with his father. He is
compared to his brother, for whom nothing changes and who envies the
welcome the prodigal receives. Rather than condemn boldness, Jesus sees
it as a sign of spiritual health. Those who paralyze the human spirit and
condemn its manifestations commit the far greater sin. They deny their
own energies and let them fester, to do much damage in the long run.

Psychotherapy reveals that sins of omission present a far greater
problem in most cases than sins of commission. Most of us are like the
paralytic with lives and emotions so bottled up, so restrained and paralyzed, that healthy expression is thwarted. Such people need to be more
open to their feelings and emotions. Doing so enables them to have richer,
more honest relationships and to tap new creative energy. Releasing such
energies often brings a better sense of life's meaning, as well as wisdom to
guide this new self-expression. By recognizing our inhibitions and becoming morally responsible for them, we live more creatively. The Pharisees

represent an ultimately immoral religious standpoint because they never faced their true nature and their resentment of Jesus.

Sinning in the eyes of the Pharisees may thus offer an experience of God's healing power. This does not give moral license, as the Pharisees feared, but heightened moral responsibility and a greater respect for individual freedom of choice. Judgments are held in abeyance so that others may discover their own sense of religious responsibility.

Another gospel story wrestles with these issues, the story of the man at the pool of Bethzatha. It is told in John's gospel.

> Now there is in Jerusalem by the Sheep Gate a pool, in Hebrew called Bethzatha, which has five porticoes. In these lay a multitude of invalids, blind, lame, paralyzed. One man was there, who had been ill for thirty-eight years. When Jesus saw him and knew that he had been lying there a long time, he said to him, "Do you want to be healed?" The sick man answered him, "Sir, I have no man to put me into the pool when the water is troubled, and while I am going another steps down before me." Jesus said to him, "Rise, take up your pallet, and walk." And at once the man was healed, and he took up his pallet and walked.
>
> Now that day was the sabbath. So the Jews said to the man who was cured, "It is the sabbath; it is not lawful for you to carry your pallet." But he answered them, "The man who healed me said to me, 'Take up your pallet, and walk.' " They asked him, "Who is the man who said to you, 'Take up your pallet, and walk'?" Now the man who had been healed did not know who it was, for Jesus had withdrawn, as there was a crowd in the place. Afterward, Jesus found him in the temple, and said to him, "See, you are well! Sin no more, that nothing worse befall you." The man went away and told the Jews that it was Jesus who had healed him. And this was why the Jews persecuted Jesus, because he did this on the sabbath. But Jesus answered them, "My Father is working still, and I am working." This was why the Jews sought all the more to kill him, because he not only broke the sabbath but also called God his own Father, making himself equal to God (Jn 5:2–18).

Some Bible translations include a legend that helps explain why the man sat at the pool for so long. It extends verse three and adds a verse, as follows:

In these lay a multitude of invalids, blind, lame, paralyzed waiting for the moving of the water; for an angel of the Lord went
down at certain seasons into the pool, and troubled the water:
whoever stepped in first after the troubling of the water was
healed of whatever disease he had (Jn 5:3b–4).[9]

From the description of those at the pool and the reference to the
man's pallet, most likely this man was also paralytic. The issues in his
healing are very similar to those in the previous story. John offers further
nuances. He is concerned with healing and religion as well as with healing
and sin. The elements of his story indicate that healing requires deeper
religious experience than the Pharisees offer. John likes to emphasize how
long the people Jesus heals have been ill and tells us that this man has been
ill thirty-eight years.

The story leading off the previous chapter of John's gospel sets up the
development of this one. Jesus meets a Samaritan woman at a well and
asks her for a drink. She is surprised that he, a Jew, would have anything to
do with her, a Samaritan and a woman. Her surprise increases when she
discovers that Jesus knows that she has had five husbands. Jesus tells her
that they who drink the water of the well will thirst again, but that he can
offer "a spring of water welling up to eternal life" (Jn 4:14b). Then John
recounts the healing of the official's son at Capernaum. Both of these
stories serve to introduce the healing at Bethzatha. The reader is led to
anticipate that this man who cannot get into the pool will possibly be led to
the living water that Jesus has been talking about.[10]

When Jesus realizes that the man has lain there a long time, he asks,
"Do you want to be healed?" He must be clear where the man is. Is he
feeding on the attention his condition brings him, or does he want to face
the challenges of healing? The paralytic explains that he has been unable
to get to the water before someone else. He does want to be healed, and
after thirty-eight years he has not despaired of this possibility. He explains
that he has no one to put him into the water, no mediator to facilitate the
healing process. Jesus does not lead him to the waters of the pool, however.
Rather, he leads him to those inner waters he described to the Samaritan
woman. Jesus gives him the same instruction as the paralytic in Mark:
"Rise, take up your pallet, and walk." The man does so, cured. He did not
need contact with the pool after all. Like the first paralytic, his cure depends both on Jesus' mediation and on his own desire for new life.

The latter part of the story introduces important dimensions of healing related to both religion and sin. The man by the pool develops much as the man born blind did. John informs us that it was on the sabbath that this man was healed. When the Jews (equivalent to the scribes and Pharisees in the synoptic gospels) see the man carrying his pallet, they ask him why, for to them it is against the law. Until now the man probably never realized that he was transgressing the law. After being cured, he took up his pallet in response to Jesus' instructions. Now he must choose between following those instructions and putting the pallet down. He chooses the former. "The man who healed me said to me, 'Take up your pallet, and walk.' "

Afterward, in the temple, Jesus makes a most important statement to the man: "See, you are well! Sin no more, that nothing worse befall you." The Greek *hugies,* here translated as "well," has the broad sense of being healthy, sound, whole, not just in body but *in toto.* The health Jesus now perceives in the man has more to do with the confident way he held his ground with the Pharisees, an act of psychological health, than with the cure of his paralysis. This is borne out by Jesus' instruction to sin no more. His condition is spiritual as well as physical, the sin one not of commission but of omission. Now that he can speak and live more boldly, he exhibits physical, psychological, and spiritual health.

After this encounter, the man went away and told the Jews that Jesus had healed him. Once again we hear of their defensive, hostile reaction. In their spiritual paralysis, they could not bear to think of Jesus doing healing work. Nor did they like it when those who were healed stood up to them. They used the fact that the healing took place on the sabbath to persecute Jesus. Jesus told them, "My Father is working still, and I am working." This means that God is working for healing, and Jesus, doing his will, is also working for healing. While Jesus related to God as Father, he taught his disciples to relate to him the same way. He taught them, for example, to pray by saying, "Our Father." Jesus never claimed an exclusive relationship to God. God was available to any individual. But, as we have seen, the Pharisees (Jews) tended to misinterpret him, projecting their own sense of exclusive relationship to God onto Jesus. They missed the opportunity (for thirty-eight years) to help the paralytic establish a closeness to God, because they were much more distant from God than they cared to realize. So they sought to kill Jesus for a sin, spiritual pride or hubris, that was really their own, a sin that often left others paralyzed physically, spiritually, and psychologically.

This story concludes on a note sounded in all four gospels. God is always working for healing in our lives. When we respond to him, we can hasten the healing process. Each of us who is furthering God's healing work is a true child of God, and can rightly call him "Father."

This paralytic's desire to be healed, his strength in speaking directly to the Jews, and his courage in carrying his pallet demonstrates that the individual's inner resolve is an important aspect of healing. We will explore this resolve further in the next chapter, as we consider the relationship between healing and faith.

NOTES

[1] Parallels in Mt 9:1-8 and Lk 5:17-26.

[2] Also see Mk 4:21, Mt 5:15, 6:22-23, and Lk 11:33-36 for teachings of Jesus that reflect the importance of consciousness, and Mt 10:26-28 and Lk 12:2-5 for teachings that indicate that all that is hidden must become known.

[3] Also see Pss 25:16-18, 32:5, 85:2 and Jer 31:34 for other Old Testament references to the forgiveness of sin.

[4] For example, see the parable of the prodigal son (Lk 15:11-32) and Jesus' comments about a group of people executed by the Romans and another group killed in an accident (Lk 13:1-5).

[5] See also Lk 11:46.

[6] Lk 7:36-50.

[7] Jn 8:2-11:7.

[8] Lk 15:11-32.

[9] This text is found in footnote K on page 1292 of *The New Oxford Annotated Bible*.

[10] Water is often a symbol for healing, and Jung points out that it is a universal symbol for the unconscious, the source of our psychic life. The symbol of water often appears in people's dreams when they begin to work on their inner life or begin to deal with psychological or physical symptoms. Frequently people find themselves in dreams setting up a house by the ocean or in other ways coming close to the sea. Such dreams affirm that if healing is going to unfold, then the individual must move into closer relationship to his unconscious.

Chapter 8
Healing and Faith

Journeying to the home of one of the rulers of the synagogue, Jesus encounters a woman who seeks healing. This is how Mark reports the event:

> And a great crowd followed him and thronged about him. And there was a woman who had had a flow of blood for twelve years, and who suffered much under many physicians, and had spent all that she had, and was no better but rather grew worse. She had heard the reports about Jesus, and came up behind him in the crowd and touched his garment. For she said, "If I touch even his garments, I shall be made well." And immediately the hemorrhage ceased; and she felt in her body that she was healed of her disease. And Jesus, perceiving in himself that power had gone forth from him, immediately turned about in the crowd, and said, "Who touched my garments?" And his disciples said to him, "You see the crowd pressing around you, and yet you say, 'Who touched me?'" And he looked around to see who had done it. But the woman, knowing what had been done to her, came in fear and trembling and fell down before him, and told him the whole truth. And he said to her, "Daughter, your faith has made you well; go in peace, and be healed of your disease" (Mk 5:24b–34).

This woman's situation resembles that of some people in our own culture who go to doctors for healing and cannot find it.[2] Their discouragement often makes their illness worse. Women in particular run into this difficulty. Some feminist literature addresses the special problem of women who seek healing from what is primarily a male-oriented profession.[3] Their experiences and the one in the gospel are not an indictment of the medical profession and what it offers; rather, they demonstrate the limits of medical science and call our attention to the *non*-medical aspects of healing which are numerous and largely ignored. Both in Jesus' time and in our own, for all the advances of medical science, the majority of doctors are not comfortable with the emotional and spiritual aspects of healing. No passage in the gospels suggests that Jesus criticized physicians, but some present evidence of their limitations.

The woman in this story knew no others besides physicians from whom to seek healing. For twelve years they could do nothing, for sometimes with physical illness non-physical factors are at work, with which physicians are not equipped to deal.[4] Convinced of the rightness of their methods, very likely they could offer the woman no other options. Like others who sought Jesus for healing, she suffered more than physically. As with the lepers, her illness probably made her ritually unclean, cutting her off from her religious community and making her incapable of performing her religious duties. She is left to suffer on her own resources, and without money. She hears the reports about Jesus and decides to seek him out. What is there to lose? After twelve years something deep within her is still convinced she can find healing. She approaches Jesus with simple expectations, not anticipating great action, but only wanting to touch his garment. First, she has to find him and then make her way through the crowd. Neither the distance nor the crowd would keep her from her purpose.

As the woman approaches Jesus, she repeats to herself that if she can touch even his garments, she can be made well. In no other gospel healing story does healing take place like this.[5] The inspiration for healing does not come from Jesus, the potential healer, but from within the woman seeking healing. It is her idea, given what she knows about Jesus, that she might experience healing through him. She responds to a fantasy that emerges from within her: when she acts on it and touches Jesus' garment, she feels a change in her body. Jesus is not even actively involved. The woman is healed by her response to her own inner images. Her twelve years of suffering push her to trust her own resources. Her experience parallels that of women today who must struggle to live in harmony with their monthly cycles in the midst of society's demands. Her body, with its constant flow of blood, was trying to tell her something, encouraging her to get in deeper touch with her soul and her life force, which blood often symbolizes. She finally accomplishes this through the fantasy of touching Jesus' garment. When she lives out this fantasy, the flow of blood ceases and her bodily cycles regain their natural rhythm.

Jesus becomes actively involved only after the woman is healed. His sense that energy has left him reveals his sensitivity to the subtle movements of life's healing forces. Those who heal by touch report a flow of energy moving from themselves to the person being healed.[6] This happened with Jesus even without his conscious involvement. The transfer of energy here indicates that this woman could not have approached just anyone for healing. Her fantasy was appropriate for Jesus. Likewise, in modern psychotherapy, the therapist's inner development is an important factor. The client has to "click" with the therapist so that in their dynamics there is a sense of a healing presence moving through the relationship. In a good relationship, the dreams and fantasies of the person seeking healing are stirred in a way that leads him further into his inner depths toward healing.

When the woman touches him, Jesus alone senses that something special has happened. Hers was a touch very different from the press of the crowd. When Jesus asks his disciples who touched his garments, they are incredulous. Many people are pressing against him; how can he ask such a question? This exchange points up the different levels of spiritual development exhibited by the disciples and Jesus.[7] For the time, Jesus becomes more intimately connected to this woman than he is to them. The disciples cannot comprehend a relationship that has so quickly developed, and with such depth.

Jesus knows he has been touched in a special way. Undaunted by his disciples' skepticism, he looks for the person who has touched him. The woman, meanwhile, knowing what has happened to her, comes to him in fear and trembling. She falls down before him and tells him the whole truth. This profound experience has obviously deeply moved her. She has searched so long for healing that its sudden manifestation takes her by surprise. A great emotional release emerges, so deep it shakes her to the core. With complete honesty she tells Jesus everything that has happened to her. This phase of healing can be compared with what psychotherapists call *catharsis*. Usually it is the first major step in psychotherapy, the precursor to real healing. A side of each of us wants to hold back and not reveal the truth about ourselves, but something in the healing process insists that we do. People can be in psychotherapy for years before they allow themselves to share with the therapist some long-hidden truth. In this woman's case, the catharsis comes at the point where she touches her emotional depths in a new way and the physical symptom disappears. Because Jesus has been so alert to the way she touched his garment, he is the recipient of this release. Amid the pressing crowd, he provides comfort and understanding.

In his final words to the woman, Jesus sums up her entire experience. He says to her, "Daughter, your faith has made you well; go in peace, and be healed of your disease." As he did with the paralytic lowered to him through the roof, Jesus addresses this woman in an intimate way. By calling her "daughter" he recognizes her vulnerable position. He offers her a personal conversation in the midst of the crowd and the general unawareness of what is happening. He tells her that her faith has made her well and brought her to health. Faith pushed her to seek healing even after the normal channels and resources had been exhausted. Faith moved her to seek out this man she had heard rumors about and to respond to her own fantasy of touching his garment. As she lies exhausted before Jesus, she can now go forward in peace. She has discovered a new ground for living.

Then Jesus tells her to be healed of her disease. We have seen that she was healed of the physical malady when she touched Jesus' garments. His parting comment indicates that her problem was not just physical, but spiritual. The physical illness was a symptom of a deeper problem whose pain motivated her to seek a resolution. Jesus' statement implies that the catharsis was most important in healing the spiritual disease. Her physical struggle brought forth the catharsis that allowed for complete healing.

This story indicates that especially in regard to healing, faith is a unique quality of the soul, of the core of the personality.[8] Faith is not experienced through religious formulas, but in the determination and persistence that carries a person through the pain of life toward a direct experience of God. Faith is a living trust that carries the capacity to respond to the movement of God.

Another way of seeing this point is to look at how Jesus was addressed by the people he healed. There was no conformity in their perceptions of him. When Bartimaeus cried out, "Jesus, Son of David, have mercy on me," Jesus did not accept or reject the manner in which Bartimaeus addressed him. He did not discuss the meaning of the term "Son of David." Rather, Jesus responded to the boldness of Bartimaeus' proclamation and to his desire for healing.[9] The same is true in the story of the man born blind. Asked what he thinks about Jesus, this man tells the Pharisees that he is a prophet. When the man later encounters Jesus, Jesus does not try to correct this perception. He encourages him in the inspired way that he spoke to the Pharisees.[10] Theology and Christology are not important to Jesus. He is concerned with helping others find healing, in whatever way it might come. The essence of this aspect of Jesus' ministry is captured in the statement, "Why do you call me 'Lord, Lord,' and do not do what I tell you?" (Lk 6:46). None of those Jesus healed called him "Lord," or used any other common Christian designation for him. Only the Pharisees perceive Jesus as equating himself with God.[11]

A healing story found in Matthew, Luke, and John makes this point further. We will look at the version in John.[12]

> So he came again to Cana in Galilee, where he had made the water wine. And at Capernaum there was an official whose son was ill. When he heard that Jesus had come from Judea to Galilee, he went and begged him to come down and heal his son, for he was at the point of death. Jesus therefore said to him, "Unless you see signs and wonders you will not believe." The official said to him, "Sir, come down before my child dies." Jesus said to him, "Go; your son will live." The man believed the word that Jesus spoke to him and went his way. As he was going down, his servants met him and told him that his son was living. So he asked them the hour when he began to mend, and they said to him, "Yesterday at the seventh hour the fever left him." The father knew that was the hour when Jesus had said to him, "Your son will live"; and he himself believed, and all his household (Jn 4:46–53).[13]

In all three accounts this healing takes place at Capernaum. John gives the general reference of an official whose son is ill. Matthew and Luke say it was a centurion's slave. The other stories in the gospels with parent-child healing lead me to believe that John is probably more accurate.[14] The healing of a servant through intervention of the master might be more dramatic than the healing of a child through the intervention of a parent, but the latter is much more likely. We saw in Chapter 2 that both Matthew and Luke have a strong inclination to embellish Jesus' healing. John begins his version of the story addressing this issue. When the man approaches Jesus, he beseeches him to come to his home to heal his son. Jesus says to him, "Unless you see signs and wonders you will not believe." He does not heal to do something extraordinary and spectacular. This is not what his ministry is about, nor what a life lived on real faith is based on. Faith or belief based on tall stories or hopes of things so unusual they are out of touch with life as God created it will not lead us very far, for such faith does not nourish and feed the depths of the soul. Jesus doesn't heal so that people will believe; he supports genuine faith as the necessary ingredient of healing.

In the story the man shows courage, boldness, and compassion on behalf of his child. Perceiving these qualities, Jesus sees potential for health for his son and he tells him so. The man gains confidence as they speak and believes what Jesus tells him. Jesus does nothing for the boy directly, but he does great things in a simple way for the father. Returning to his son, the father finds that the boy is mending and his fever gone. He notes that the fever left at the same time Jesus told him his son would live—the very moment when he himself came to believe it. When the burning issue of faith in this man is resolved, the fever burning in his son subsides.

Matthew and Luke also stress the role of the man's faith in the heal-ing. They indicate that this man is a non-Jew who yet showed himself very capable of the resolve necessary for healing. He lacked the religious or intellectual skepticism of the Pharisees. This and other stories in the gos-pels make clear that faith is not limited to any one religious expression or nationality. It can be found in any human soul and can assist that soul in its search for healing. It is not bound by cultural and religious conventions. Faith is a crucial element in the Gospel stories, whether they concern non-Jews like the Gerasene demoniac and the Syrophoenician woman or the many Jewish people Jesus healed. It is important not only to the person being healed, but to those intimately involved with the afflicted individual like this father.

In an interview once with the BBC's John Freeman, Jung was asked if he believed in God. He paused, remarked that the question was a difficult one to answer, and then said, "I don't believe, I know."[15] Jung's statement followed a long life of wrestling with his own soul and those of many others. As he explored the psyche of modern human beings, he found a will operating that was greater and much wiser than the will or ego of the individual. Proper response to this inner wisdom brought meaning and purpose even in the face of suffering and death. To find healing and allow this greater purpose to emerge took great courage and, in the language of the gospels, faith. Mere belief in religious formulas was not enough. The courage of true faith is required if a person is to seek healing and en-counter God.

Jung's wrestling with the difference between mere belief and faith went back to his childhood. His father was a Swiss Reform minister whose insistence on blind belief in Christian doctrine irked Jung from an early age. Jung felt that religion had to be more than that; it was something to be experienced. He felt that his father's belief system was a defense from a living encounter with God and his own inner depths. At age eleven something brought this to the forefront. A horrible thought began breaking into his consciousness, which he knew to be a great sin. He resisted it for days, but suffered great anxiety. Finally he decided that since he did not want the thought, it must come from God. Reflections on Adam and Eve helped him come to this resolution. Jung's thought was an image of the divine destruction of a great local cathedral. The young boy learned that God often asks us to do the very thing we most fear in order to live out the divine will. When Jung let the thought come to him, he was filled with a profound sense of grace and the presence of God. (We recall the struggle of Abraham when God asks him to sacrifice his son, Isaac.) Jung became convinced, even at age eleven, that God could ask us to go against all convention, even religious convention, to have direct knowledge of him.[16] The parable of the prodigal son reminds us that it was the restless, way-ward son, not the dutiful son, who received the deepest love and forgive-ness from the father (Lk 15:11–32).

When we recognize that Jung's early experience came to the son of a clergyman before the turn of the century, we can fully appreciate its intensity. But if Jung had not allowed the dark fantasy to come, there is no telling what tension and stress he would have suffered. Jung trusted coura-geously in what wanted to emerge in him. While he did not exhibit the conventional faith of his day, he exhibited an extraordinary faith in God. Later, when he faced his most intense inner wrestling, from which emerged the very core of his psychology, it was this same faith, courage, and trust in the divine that allowed him to see it through.[17] His early experience was instrumental in getting through the much longer, more difficult adult experience. Jung's personal encounters exemplify the faith seen in the gospels. His is a psychology founded on faith.

Faith appears on many levels and in many forms. It is necessary for any kind of healing—medical, psychological, or spiritual. When healing takes place, it has as much to do with the person being healed as with the healer. Jerome Frank, a modern-day doctor, has done some very interest-ing studies of healing.[18] Frank reports that before the advent of penicillin medical doctors were actually faith healers, but didn't know it. Patients' belief and trust in their doctors made them well more than anything the physicians did. More recently, Frank reports, the success of drugs and surgery is due to a great extent to the placebo effect.[19] These medical procedures work because patients trust that they will. Anthropologists and other researchers studying shamanistic healing have at times scoffed at these healers because some have faked the removal of a foreign object from the patient. But the shamans were not performing actual surgery. They enacted the ritual, "magical" removal of a destructive foreign object from the patient's body for the sake of its positive emotional impact on the individual. Debunking this kind of healing actually undermines the patient's faith mechanism and lowers the chances for healing.

When we go to our doctors today, much of their success is due to our trust. They become the bearers of the healing agent within our own souls and bodies. The same is true when we consult other professionals, like psychotherapists and clergy. Faith and trust activate the healing process. Of course consulting just anyone will not always work, as we saw in the story of the woman with the flow of blood. The choice of the person consulted for healing makes a difference, depending on how much he or she helps or discourages healing. Important as their own faith was, the people who consulted Jesus might not have found healing if their faith had not led them to the right person.

Many times one professional can bring healing where another has failed. Persistence in seeking healing is very important. Probably the most dramatic situations of this kind involve people suffering from life-threatening diseases whose doctors tell them that they have no chance for recovery. Such a prognosis will not promote healing, but some individuals refuse to accept it. They do not lose faith along with the medical practitioner. Their hope for healing moves them to seek other alternatives and possibly complete recovery. Examples from the gospels and from lives today indicate that faith can indeed lead us to healing.[20] However, the faith that allows this healing to happen is not expressed in traditional religious ideology.

The story of the Syrophoenician woman, which we examined in Chapter 3, provides further insight on the importance of faith in healing (Mk 7:24–30). We recall that this woman, a non-Jew, came to Jesus requesting that he cast a demon out of her daughter. Jesus' response as she fell at his feet was, "Let the children first be fed, for it is not right to take the children's bread and throw it to the dogs." Jesus tells this woman that his ministry is only to the children of Israel; therefore, he will not get involved with a non-Jew like her. As he tries to put her off, the woman persists and responds, "Yes, Lord; yet even the dogs under the table eat the children's crumbs." This woman will not be rebuffed. She recognizes in Jesus someone with the capacity for healing, and something deep in her is stirred. She picks up the image of the crumbs and the dog and gives it back to him with new meaning. Something in her is bent on making a connection with him despite his pushing her away. She could very well have gotten angry over the reference to non-Jews as dogs and gone off in a huff. Instead, she plays with the image and makes a remarkable reply. Like the woman with a hemorrhage, this woman persists in her quest. From the depths of her imagination comes the impetus for healing.

Jesus' response is no less remarkable. He tells her, "For this saying you may go your way; the demon has left your daughter." Recognizing her extraordinary reaction to his words, Jesus is so impressed that he changes his entire attitude to his call from God. In his early years Jesus saw his ministry as only to the people of Israel. Through this experience it changed to include everyone he encountered. His meeting with the Syrophoenician woman had a great deal to do with this expansion of his healing work. Jesus sees in her and others the key quality needed for healing and transformation: faith. He discovered that a deep faith could live in any soul regardless of the outer religious articulation of belief.

We can further appreciate Jesus' response to his woman when we consider what he might have replied—or what the Pharisees might have replied. He could have persisted in dismissing her. After all, was he not the one with the great healing ability? Who was she to challenge him? The Pharisees would have reiterated to her that she was not of their chosen race. Besides, women were not to speak to men like that. Did she not know her place? Jesus demonstrates a most important quality of the healer: openness to what emerges from the soul. Throughout the gospels Jesus shows an extraordinary responsiveness to women, especially when they speak from their honest feelings. Psychologically, we might say he was very open to the feminine side of life, as expressed both in women and himself. This relationship to the feminine is crucial to the nurturing of the soul and to healing.[21]

Moreover, an established healer or teacher can become fixed in his approach to illness and health, full of professional superiority toward those who come for healing and growth. Jesus demonstrates that no matter how well developed we are, we need an attitude that allows new aspects of life to emerge into our consciousness. This is also vital to our relationships. For we are struggling to be open not only to the images that emerge from our own soul, but also to those coming from the souls of others. Each speaks a unique truth. Considering the change it works in both people, the meeting of Jesus with the Syrophoenician woman is one of the most significant human encounters in the gospels.

This story also demonstrates the importance of feminine psychology to healing. Such a psychology does not refer exclusively to women, but to a feminine principle equally relevant to the development of men. In putting off the Syrophoenician woman, Jesus refers to non-Jews as dogs—household beasts to which one would not throw the bread meant for children. The woman pursues this image, stating that even dogs have the good sense to eat the crumbs under the table. (Knowing how children eat, there would be lots of crumbs.) In this clever response, the woman reminds Jesus of his own experience. Many of the children of Israel, especially those dogmatically bound by their religious laws, were not allowing themselves to be spiritually fed. They were disconnected from that natural instinct, symbolized by the dog, which would not hesitate to fulfill its basic needs.

We could say that it was the "dog nature" of the woman with a hemorrhage that led her to sniff along until she found what her soul required. The Syrophoenician woman followed similar instincts in her conversation with Jesus. Like the dog, faith is earthy and instinctive. It is not mental, analytical, dogmatic, and legalistic, as organized religion tends to make it, for such faith cannot heal.

The image of the dog arises quite often today in the fairy tales, myths, and dreams of feminine psychology. A good example from my practice is that of a woman wrestling with issues in her personal and spiritual life. She dreamed that she was in a great cathedral. She had to go to the bathroom and returned home to do so. Then she returned to the cathedral with her dog. They did not go back inside, since the dog was not allowed, so they sniffed around outside. As we discussed the dream, it was clear that this woman could not express an important part of herself in her church life. She had to do so within her own self, symbolized by her home. If she was going to relate to the church, it had to be through her dog—her inner instinctive nature—even though the dog might not be accepted. This dream occurred at a time when the woman was acquiring a deeper sense both of what attracted her to the church and of how this institution did *not* fit into her own spiritual development.

This woman's experience parallels that of the Syrophoenician woman. Her response to the dog imagery enabled Jesus to perceive more fully the exclusivity and Pharisaism of his own religion. There should be no obstacle to any soul's search for healing, he realized. The dream of the dog and the cathedral calls to mind Jung's boyhood experience with the cathedral in his home town. His vision also made it clear that God would not be bound by human religious institutions. Real faith does not lead to Pharisaism and self-righteousness, but to knowledge of God and to healing. Faith is a movement of the soul, its lifeblood. It keeps the soul from a passive existence based only on belief. In the next chapter we will look more closely at where faith, as seen in the gospel healing stories, leads us.

NOTES

¹ Parallels are found in Mt 9:20–22 and Lk 8:42b–48.

² For two modern examples see Cousins, *The Anatomy of an Illness,* Chapter 1, and Albert Kreinheder, "The Healing Power of Illness."

³ See *Our Bodies, Ourselves* by the Boston Women's Health Collective and *Hygieia, A Woman's Herbal* by Jeannine Parvati.

⁴ Modern depth psychology began because the medical approach was inadequate in treating certain illnesses that were successfully treated by psychological means. Jung begins his article "Psychology and Religion" by giving examples of such instances (*Psychology and Religion: West and East,* CW, Vol. 11, pp. 5–23).

⁵ While this does not happen in any of the other major healing stories we are discussing, there are a few general references to others touching Jesus and being healed. See, for example, Mk 3:10–12 and Mt 6:56.

⁶ Agnes Sanford, *The Healing Light.*

⁷ Recall the inability of the disciples to heal the boy possessed by a spirit, Mk 9:14–29, discussed in Chapter 3.

⁸ See John Sanford, *The Kingdom Within,* Chapter 8, "The Faith of the Soul," for amplification of Jesus' teachings concerning this important inner quality.

⁹ Mk 10:46–52, discussed in Chapter 6.

¹⁰ Jn 9, discussed in Chapter 6.

¹¹ For example, see our discussion of Mk 2:1–12 in Chapter 7.

¹² Somehow the original story was left out of Mark, so we have less sense of what the actual experience might have been. Matthew, Luke, and John seem to tell the story to fit the slant of their gospels. I choose John's because he stays closer to the general implications of the healing stories than do Matthew and Luke.

¹³ Synoptic versions are found in Mt 8:5–13 and Lk 7:1–10.

¹⁴ Mk 5:21–24, 35–43 (the healing of Jairus' daughter), Mk 7:24–30 (the healing of the Syrophoenician woman's daughter) and Mk 9:14–29 (the healing of the boy possessed by a spirit). The records of Mark indicate parent-child healing is common and make no mention of the healing of a

106   *Transforming Body and Soul*

slave through a master's intervention. I believe the shift we see in Matthew and Luke to include a slave is their addition to the healing record rather than historical. In this case we see the earlier version maintained only by John.

[15] "Face to Face," BBC interview of Jung by John Freeman.

[16] C.G. Jung, *Memories, Dreams, Reflections,* pp. 36–43.

[17] Ibid., Chapter 6, "Confrontation with the Unconscious," pp. 170–99.

[18] Jerome D. Frank, *Persuasion and Healing.*

[19] Frank, "The Medical Power of Faith."

[20] To mention only two: Norman Cousins' story told in the first chapter of *Anatomy of an Illness* and Albert Kreinheder's story told in "The Healing Power of Illness." Also, I am particularly grateful to Barbara Coleman for sharing her experiences. Twenty years ago Barbara discovered that she had a malignant brain tumor. Doctors told her that she would probably not live long. Through psychotherapy and other means, in addition to medical treatment, Barbara was able to make a full recovery despite the initial pessimistic predictions. Now her doctors have given her a clean bill of health and see no prospects for remission. Barbara has founded a cancer support system "We Can Do!" based in Arcadia, California.

[21] For men this is connected to what Jung called the anima, the feminine aspect of their personality. The soul of both men and women seems to be of a feminine nature. See Irene Claremont de Castillejo, *Knowing Woman,* Chapter 11, for a discussion of soul from the perspective of a woman's psychology.

Chapter 9
Healing and the Way

We find two kinds of healing in the gospels. Sometimes there is a cure—the person is changed and his symptoms are eliminated. Other times an important extra dimension emerges that pushes the person to continue growing in a unique, personal way. It is with the second group that we are concerned here. To certain people, Jesus makes a parting statement like this one: "Go your way, your faith has made you well" (Mk 10:52a). As we have just seen, such people have a quality of faith that leads them to seek more than physical health. The most important part of Jesus' dismissal, though, is the directive to "go your way." Jesus does not say "come my way" or "go out and tell everyone about me." These people have reached a point where they must follow the life path God has given them. This does not mean that they can go out and live as they please, but rather that they are now in a position to grow beyond the realm of physical health alone. They are presented with the opportunity to choose the way of life God intends for them.

In certain such cases, healing involves coming to terms with God's meaning and purpose. As we recognize and accept this purpose, transformation occurs. Jung called this process *individuation,* the means by which we each become the complete personality we are meant to be.[1] This is the soul's deepest urge, Jung believed, through which true meaning and purpose unfold. He relates the process of individuation to the life of Jesus: "It is no easy matter to live a life that is modeled on Christ's, but it is unspeakably harder to live one's own life as truly as Christ lived his."[2]

The gospel healing stories indicate that not all who are healed by Jesus find their "way" in this sense. They may show elements of having done so, perhaps an increased consciousness, but healing alone, or a state of health, does not guarantee one is following God's way. The leper healed in Mark is a good example: he gets carried away with himself and does not heed Jesus' instructions, missing an opportunity for further growth and development.[3] Luke, describing the healing of ten lepers, contrasts the different responses that followed the event.[4] All ten men have enough faith to be healed, but only one, the Samaritan, has the depth of faith to find his own way and to grow spiritually. The other nine could become ill again, if not with leprosy, then with some other physical or psychological ailment. They will not pursue the meaning of their lives any further than they deem necessary. The Samaritan, by contrast, takes on the burden of living his life as fully as possible.

The story of the Syrophoenician woman indicates that one need not be Jewish or Christian to find one's way. (Augustine hinted at the same things in his *City of God*.) We have already seen this woman's extraordinary faith, a natural quality of soul and not a product of culture or religion. Her heartfelt response to Jesus creates the opportunity for her to find her special call, but that call will not be to follow Jesus. This story has profound implications for Christian evangelism, namely, that Christian ministry should be directed primarily to healing souls and bodies, not to requirements of membership and adherence to particular beliefs. Healing is a gift from God available to any soul who searches for it.

While John does not speak directly of "the way," he has his own nuances for this process. The man born blind, for example, pursues his healing beyond the cure itself and finds the way to fuller spiritual development.[5] Besides Jesus, no one in the gospels speaks more eloquently in the presence of the Pharisees than this man. His words are obviously inspired by God. Afterward, Jesus points out to the man that it is the Son of man who speaks to him. The mythological image of the Son of man, which Jesus so often referred to, can be seen as depicting the process of finding one's own way. Since Jesus always referred to the Son of man in the third person, most likely he used this mythological figure to refer to his own development and relationship with God and suggested it as such to others. Following the resurrection, Jesus' own life became the pattern of individuation for the first Christians. His story replaced that of the Son of man.[6]

The story of Bartimaeus points to the foundation of the Christian life. After Jesus says to Bartimaeus, "Go your way; your faith has made you well," Mark tells us that Bartimaeus received his sight and followed Jesus on "the way." "The way" was an early term for the followers of Christ.[7] This context indicates that it was comprised of individuals like Bartimaeus, who were responding to their own God-given way—as Jesus himself was doing. We have already described Bartimaeus as an individual trying to express his true self.[8] He shows "heart," a closeness to his deepest feelings. After his healing, he will no longer wear the mantle imposed on him by society. He is a good candidate for "the way."

Jesus' life as outlined in the gospels can be seen as a paradigm of the transformation necessary for an individual to find his way.[9] The teachings of Jesus describe this process.[10] The transformation of those who come to him for healing calls our attention to an important point: Jesus could heal as much as he did because *he himself was going his God-given way.* He did not teach and heal in order to build up a reputation; rather, his teaching and healing came from following God's will. Our way is something God creates. The individual strives to participate in this process consciously. For the Christian, the way is symbolized by the cross, a reminder that in following God's will, like Jesus, one must encounter suffering and death. The spiritual way is not meant to be an escape from these things. It does not bring a comfortable existence with all our earthly needs provided for.

Jesus did not suffer on the cross alone. He had to endure the slow development of his disciples and the great resistance of the Pharisees. He had to wrestle with the great needs of so many he encountered and his inability to satisfy them all. These and many other tensions are part of following the way. Each of us must carry certain tensions, especially the pull between what we want for our life and what God intends for it. Jesus teaches through his healing ministry that not all suffering has to be endured. Much of our bodily suffering can be transformed as we come to understand its purpose. Often our symptoms are relieved when we learn to live through inner tension properly.

Jesus did not go the way of the cross to spare us from doing so ourselves. This common misconception greatly distorts the inner life and limits our own healing work. Jesus went the way of the cross so that we could do so more courageously. "If any man would come after me, let him deny himself and take up his cross and follow me" (Mk 8:34b). Nothing takes the place of finding our way, certainly not mere religious proclamation. "Why do you call me 'Lord, Lord,' and not do what I tell you?" (Lk 6:46) Extraordinary spiritual gifts are not enough. They may even deflect us from the way. "Not every one who says to me, 'Lord, Lord,' shall enter the kingdom of heaven, but he who does the will of my Father who is in heaven. On that day many will say to me, 'Lord, Lord, did we not prophesy in your name, and cast out demons in your name, and do many mighty works in your name?'" And then I will declare to them, 'I never knew you; depart from me, you evildoers' " (Mt 7:21–23).

No one else can go our way for us. We can receive support, guidance, and insight from others. We can reflect and meditate on our spiritual heritage, but we must live and choose our way for ourselves. This means we must come to *see* God's way for us instead of our own. Individuation is a living, dynamic process. We are never there; new dimensions of our way can develop at any time.

The gospel healing stories teach not only important lessons about healing, but important means of finding God's way. They remind us of the variety of voices within us. We must discern which voices will lead us ahead on the way and which will lead us off it. Those with special spiritual gifts or who sense a special relationship with God are precisely those who need most to listen to the voices within, as Jesus did in the wilderness. Sometimes our voices may make us ill; then we are most likely to become aware of them. If we are not careful, we run the danger of getting caught by them much like the Pharisees. We have seen how important discernment of our inner voices is for healing, and it is equally important for any who would respond to God's way.

Just as healing comes when we realize the collective burdens placed on us by family, church, or society, so does the door open for finding our way. Since by definition it will differ from anyone else's way, we should be careful to avoid inappropriate comparisons. We have seen how important this is, especially within the religious community itself. Non-religious people did not oppose what Jesus was doing; the religious leaders did. The Pharisees were the strongest objectors to Jesus' work. Ironically, religious systems then and now often present the biggest obstacles to individuals who seek to hear the voice of God and their own divine call.

As we have seen, a proper sense of sin is critical for healing. It is also extremely important for individuation. What institutional religion considers sinful can influence a person's health and capacity to find the way. A perfectly acceptable religious practice might prove detrimental to some individual's health and keep him from finding his way. More and more modern people are finding that they cannot express enough of themselves in current worship services. One man, for example, dreamed that he must enter a church as a cougar, despite the threat of being killed if he did so. Both healing and finding our way require special spiritual awareness—going beyond the thinking of the time to acquire a personal sense of life's meaning. No one achieves such consciousness easily; it grows and develops as we understand how God transforms human life. We recall, for example, how Jesus' encounter with the Syrophoenician woman changed his sense of his own ministry and broadened his awareness of life. If our consciousness does not continue to expand, it is a sign that somehow we have gotten off the path.

Finally, the gospel healing stories indicate that just as healing often requires a faith rooted in the deepest yearnings of the soul, so too does the soul's journey to find its way. This faith is not a mere statement of beliefs or trust that God will care for us. We need instead a deep trust in God's presence in us, a faith that empowers us to move forth courageously. Jesus' acceptance of the cross is the primary example.

The qualities depicted in the gospels as being of great importance to a healing ministry are also extremely important to the individual seeking to find his spiritual way. The absence of a vital healing ministry in today's churches reflects a spiritual barrenness. A lot of work needs to be done. Our attitudes to God's movement in our lives need to grow and develop. Jesus never says, "Go your way, your faith has made you well," to anyone he has not healed, including the disciples. The disciples did not live their faith courageously until after they had lived through Jesus' death and resurrection. The gospels indicate, on the other hand, that some of the people Jesus healed were the farthest along the spiritual way.[11] Their illnesses played an important role in their spiritual growth and development. From the perspective of healing and the spiritual life, it is important to consider the meaning of illness and its role in finding our way. To this subject we now turn.

NOTES

[1] C.G. Jung, *Psychological Types,* pp. 448–50. Other references to individuation can be found throughout Jung's writing.

[2] Jung, *Modern Man in Search of a Soul,* p. 236.

[3] Mk 1:40–45; discussed in Chapter 4.

[4] Lk 17:11–19; discussed in Chapter 5.

[5] Jn 9; discussed in Chapter 6.

[6] Frederick H. Borsch, *The Son of Man in Myth and History,* Chapter 9.

[7] References to Christianity as "the way" are found in Acts 9:2; 18:25–26; 19:9, 23; 22:4; 24:14, 22.

[8] See Chapter 6.

[9] See Edward F. Edinger, "Christ as Paradigm of the Individuated Ego," in *Ego and Archetype.*

[10] See John A. Sanford, *The Kingdom Within.*

[11] In his teaching Jesus indicates his special relationship to the sick. "Those who are well have no need of a physician, but those who are sick" (Mk 2:17b). Parallels are found in Mt 9:12b and Lk 5:31.

Chapter 10
The Meaning of Illness

O ne of the first healing stories in Mark's gospel is the healing of Simon's mother-in-law:

> And immediately he left the synagogue, and entered the house of Simon and Andrew, with James and John. Now Simon's mother-in-law lay sick with a fever, and immediately they told him of her. And he came and took her by the hand and lifted her up, and the fever left her; and she served them (Mk 1:29–31).[1]

The story is short and seemingly straightforward. At first glance one might wonder if Jesus had healed the woman so she would be able to get up and serve them. However, we have seen that people are not healed, even by Jesus, unless they *want* to be healed. Thus something must have happened in the woman herself while Jesus was there, enough to bring about a cure. This is not unusual. In his article "Psychology and Religion," Jung reports the healing of a woman with a fever in a few minutes after she confessed the psychological cause.[2] Something very similar probably happened with Simon's mother-in-law.

Earlier in this chapter, in a well-known passage, Jesus called the four disciples he brought to Simon's house, asking all four of them to leave their fishing and go with him. This could not have pleased Simon's mother-in-law, who was concerned naturally about how he would support her daughter. But since theirs was a very patriarchal society and it was Simon's and Andrew's house, she probably didn't feel it her place to speak out. Nevertheless what was burning inside her had to be expressed, so it appeared through her body. Most likely Jesus sensed that the fever was a sign of something else and gave her the chance to articulate it when they met. Once she had been heard and taken seriously, she could go about her daily tasks—not happy, perhaps, but at least relieved of the burden of her feeling and distress. Jesus' taking her by the hand indicates the personal nature of his approach.

This little story gives a good indication of the basic function of illness. Illness uses the body to express inner conflict and gives a person a chance to become aware of it. We neglect some important psychological aspect of our existence, so the body expresses it for us. Many of our colds and flus are the action of our bodies asking us to slow down, relax, and do more inner reflection. Research today links numerous illnesses to our psychological state—from ulcers to heart attacks, from skin ailments to cancer. We realize more and more that illness is not merely the breakdown of the body, but an indication of some psychological condition. When we understand this aspect of illness and deal with it, it brings about healing. This was Jesus' approach.

In each of the gospel healing stories, people find levels of self-expression and develop greater consciousness. For some illness gives the impetus for a journey of faith that helps them to discover God's purpose. The stories we have reviewed show that the healing of Jesus involved much more than the removal of physical symptoms. People of that time had a negative attitude toward illness. The writers of the Old Testament sensed that it was connected to our relationship with God, but they did not understand how. Jesus brought a new religious attitude toward illness. He understood the meaning of illness so profoundly that he could bring healing.

Today we have a highly developed medical approach to illness, but for the most part we lack a spiritual attitude to physical symptoms. This not only limits our full potential for healing, but hampers our understanding of the place of illness in human life. Illness is not simply some malfunction of a biological system, repairable through mechanical or chemical intervention. This is our unspoken attitude. If we are ill, we go to the doctor and take the right medicine or, if need be, undergo corrective surgery, and we believe everything will be remedied. Conveniently, such an attitude keeps us from becoming *responsible* for our illness. We do not have to ask ourselves why we got sick at this time, why this particular illness, and other important questions. And furthest from our minds is the crucial question: What is God trying to tell me?

Fortunately, doctors are becoming more aware of the other dimensions of the body's complaints. They sense the importance of the patient's attitude. They realize that generally the body seeks to heal itself and that medical science at most facilitates that process. For example, if a person breaks a leg, the doctor sets it, but the body takes over from there and brings about the healing. The doctor's job becomes one of monitoring the process, providing valuable information about the state of our bodies and possible medical solutions. But we are far more responsible for the healing than we (and many doctors) like to think. We are responsible on the simple level of following our doctor's instructions and communicating with him or her as best we can; after all, it is our body. Even more important is the work of understanding the place of the illness in our life situation. As we become more aware of what is happening to us psychologically and spiritually, we greatly help the healing work of the doctor, our bodies, and God.

A complete healing approach challenges the exclusivity of medical science and questions the religious ethos of our day. So far, the greatest commitment is found in parts of the medical community and certain schools of psychology that search for healing based on the psyche and its quest for wholeness.[3] As in Jesus' time, the religious community today is generally unaware of its potential in this area. Jung developed his psychology because he found this whole aspect missing in western life and culture. Other doctors, while not entering into the specifically spiritual side of healing, see more clearly the need to take into account emotions, attitudes toward life, and the connection between body and soul. Research demonstrates this even in the case of our most feared disease, cancer.[4]

As for religion, the capacity of a religion to heal is a good indication of its health. We saw in Chapter 1 that often the shamans of primitive tribes were called to their healing role through an initiatory illness. Through this illness they experienced a deeper spirituality through which they not only found healing for themselves but encountered sacred mysteries that could heal others.

Illness calls people to a healing ministry today. Many in the helping professions come to this work because they have experienced healing themselves, physical or spiritual. A doctor acquaintance, for example, recalls that when he was five he was seriously ill and the doctor came to his house to see him (as doctors did in those days). When he recovered he was so impressed that he determined to be a doctor when he grew up. He became an excellent surgeon. A young woman chaplain reports suffering from encephalitis in the eighth grade. While in surgery, she had an out-of-the-body experience in which she saw the doctors working on her. (We will look briefly at this kind of experience in the next chapter.) She found herself in a state of ecstatic shamanistic initiation. Through the experience, she realized that she should seek some kind of hospital ministry and become a chaplain. What was asked was not necessarily going to be easy. Most Christian churches were then only beginning to accept women as clergy, and resistance was particularly strong in the chaplaincy field. Modern religion was telling her one thing, her experience of God something quite different. But her call to this ministry—derived from her illness—gave her strength to persevere.

Shamanism and the experience of many today support the view of illness as a call to healing and service. It can also be seen as a call from God to our individual God-given way. The gospel stories indicate that illness represents not only physical imbalance, but psychological and spiritual imbalance as well. There is need for more personal development and a deeper awareness of oneself, others, and life in general. These stories remind us too that illness is a matter not only of personal imbalance, but often of cultural imbalance. Those Jesus healed were afflicted because of the way society perceived them. The consciousness and life energy they needed to grow and develop were thwarted. We have seen that the incidence of heart disease, our number-one killer, may be directly related to our discomfort with the feeling side of life. Likewise with cancer. Cancer cells are inferior cells—cells that do not develop as they normally might. It is possible that cancer is such a problem because our daily stresses and strains keep many individuals from full self-development. Profiles of cancer patients indicate that often they have difficulty expressing their emotions and creativity; they do not take care of their own needs and values.[5]

Thus our major diseases present not only medical problems but also spiritual ones. Modern medical science gives us a greater opportunity than ever before to explore the meaning of our illnesses. Remarkable surgeries and chemical treatments have been developed to sustain life. These need to be complemented by inner reflection and growth of consciousness to keep our internal problems from resurfacing later. There is a tremendous potential for misuse of medical science if our healing practices do not honor this other aspect of illness.

It is important to realize that Jesus directed his main attention to the healing of the *individual.* Even when the imbalance of society or religion contributed to the illness, the individual could find a personal center of health of a deeper, more genuine nature. Jesus' healing pointed up problems in the culture, but the basis for change lay in the individual prepared to take the initiative for personal transformation—not some grand plan for the reordering of society. Jesus showed those open to it what was available. Some accepted; others did not. Jesus left them that choice.

Illness can also be a means of avoidance. It may result from a person's inability to cope with life situations. It can present very real benefits for persons who, like Peter's mother-in-law, cannot deal directly with life's dilemmas.[6] At home, at work, or in places in life where they feel trapped, some people get sick to get the attention they need. They ask for this through sickness rather than directly, in the normal course of a relationship. Others might contract a disease for the opposite reason—to avoid relating to others, to have time alone, and not to be bothered with the demands of life.

In many ways illness can be seen as a call to new life. Indeed, people who survive serious disorders are very changed afterward. In his psychological work Jung talks of neurosis as being not the problem, but the cure. The psychological distress remains until the individual resolves the underlying situation. The neurosis is trying to tell the person something. The same can be said for many physical ailments.

Authentic healing involves psychological and spiritual risk for the healer. We have already seen the risks Jesus took in defying the Pharisees. They could not stand this challenge and killed him for it. Today many members of the medical professions scoff at shamanistic healing because it is not scientific. Their rigid attachment to the scientific approach blinds them to other avenues of healing, even in cases where medical science was not successful and some other form of healing succeeded. The same is true of people in the church. While some may speak of healing, they reject many of medicine's and psychology's contributions. They are closed to much of the reality of healing around them. In most churches there is very little healing. Theology, liturgy, evangelism, or some other aspect of church life is the main focus. As in the time of the Pharisees, the presence of an active healing ministry can be very threatening to beliefs that in truth are no longer connected to human transformation.

There is not only risk for the healer in such healing, but also for the person seeking healing. That person has to be bold enough to accept personal transformation. Most people who come into psychotherapy for personal growth and development do so because they are suffering. People who do seek to change are taking a risk, for this kind of healing demands a new way of living. But for such people the price is worth it.

It is important to realize that the search for healing can lead to spiritual transformation, but not necessarily to physical health. A few years ago I saw a film on Down's syndrome featuring a young man named Rickie. His mother presented the film and talked about her experiences to the audience. When he was born, the medical establishment wanted to have Rickie placed in an institution. The mother insisted on raising him herself and giving him a normal life. Rickie developed into a fine swimmer, a real joy to his family. After the presentation the woman remarked that of all her children, she believed it was Rickie who had maximized his full potential as a person. Internal development can take place in anyone. But not in all cases does it bring full bodily health.

The Swiss Jungian analyst Adolf Guggenbühl-Craig writes in a compelling article about what he calls the Archetype of the Invalid.[7] He points out that there are limits to healing: certain types of deformity are an important part of life. They do not preclude inner development, and there is something for all of us to learn from them. Physical deformities challenge both disabled people and those in contact with them. People who carry the Archetype of the Invalid serve as God's living reminders that it is not our external health that matters most, but the health of the soul.

The gospel healing stories remind us that those who are most ill may not suffer from a physical condition. They are able-bodied, but inwardly disabled. In this sense illness is not punishment by God, but it can certainly be seen as communication from him. The people who became sick and wrestle with their ailments are the more likely to change. Others may escape illness, but like the Pharisees they make those around them pay the price for their unconscious problems. These stories remind us that even if we are not physically and psychologically ill, we have an important responsibility to live in spiritual health. By doing so we are more likely to become agents of healing to others.

Our illnesses help us continually with the work of aligning our human wills with that of God. In psychology the idea of the will is expressed by the ego, the seat of the conscious personality. The ego tends to want the world to revolve around its sense of how it would like things to be. God acts to expand ego consciousness and transform our egocentric world view.[8] The worst egocentricity, exemplified by the Pharisees, tries to use God or the spiritual life to bolster its own attitude about life. In our day such statements as "God is my co-pilot" betray this hidden egocentric spiritual attitude. The ego believes that the divine is some sort of special protector that will go along with its purposes. But in the spiritual life God is not the co-pilot. God is the pilot and we are asked to be the co-pilot. We are to bring our ego around to serving his will and purpose for us.

The stubborn human ego is easily carried away with itself. Often God needs drastic means to get its attention. Illness is one of them. Nothing stops the ego as well as an illness that prevents the body from cooperation with the ego's purposes. From this perspective the illness is more correctly seen as a *cure* to an egocentric attitude than as the problem itself. We have lost touch with one of the primary ways God speaks to us—through our bodies. It is not the only way, of course, but it is one important way. However, being free of illness does not necessarily preclude egocentricity. The ego sees bodily health as a right and the body as something that should cooperate with it. It neglects to see the body as something connecting us to the deeper life inside us and with which the ego should be cooperating. We have seen in the gospels that healing occurs when assumptions about life are challenged. When a new attitude develops, healing can take place. The bodily illness that can result when we avoid such psychological and spiritual challenges keeps the ego honest. The ego does not like pain, which often serves to motivate further development.

Here lies another danger. We assume it is our right to avoid pain and the message it may bring. This is not to say that we should all suffer needlessly, especially from excruciating pain, but it does warn us to be careful how we respond. Some health-care practitioners are becoming more aware of the value of pain in our lives.[9] Pain reminds us our bodies are trying to tell us something. Sometimes bodily pain results when the ego avoids psychic pain that it does not want to deal with. We have seen in the healing stories how illnesses of such people as the leper serve the purpose of avoiding inner psychic pain and tension. The body often responds when an individual does not deal directly with psychic distress. Avoidance is usually unconscious, so the ego does not know what is happening. The pain lets the ego become aware that there is a situation that needs its attention.

What the healing in the gospels brings to our awareness has tremendous implications for any future healing ministry. While most of medical science rejects such healings, more medical professionals are considering such work. Much of today's research is being done by such physicians, who are realizing what a great assist to their own treatment such an approach can be. A patient who is exploring the psychological and spiritual dimensions of an illness will greatly aid his or her own medical treatment. If that person's doctor encourages such work, the treatment will be that much more successful. Life becomes more alive and meaningful and not just a case of keeping the body going to meet egocentric purposes.

Ironically, the area of health care that needs to be most informed of the gospel perspective is the pastoral care of the church. Few Christians, lay or clergy, have a sense of the church as a genuine source of healing. Much prayer for healing is of the egocentric variety: "I am ill, or so-and-so is ill, God can heal, please heal me or please heal so-and-so." There is no sense of God speaking in and through the illness, or listening for God speaking through the body. The church has been reduced to a ministry of visiting the sick instead of one of healing the sick and understanding the meaning of illness. Certainly when people are sick at home and in the hospital it is good to visit and encourage them to get well. But if God is speaking to that person through the illness, then what about helping the person find the voice of God and discover a dimension of healing beyond mere medical restoration? At present the church leaves most of its healing work in the hands of other professionals, especially with physical illness. Yet the healing tradition of Jesus is almost as old as medicine itself.

Much is happening today in psychological and spiritual healing, but very little is going on in the church. The gospel ministry of healing would seem to be crucial if the church is to maintain its proper place in our society. Considering the call of Jesus to heal, the church should be a leader, not a follower, in this area. There is much Pharisaism in the church, which will need to give way in order for a vital healing ministry to take its place in active church life. This ministry should be available to people both inside and outside the church, in order to parallel the ministry of Jesus.

When authentic healing begins to take place, our spiritual lives will be fuller. The church must give up the great temptations to shore up egos that are being challenged by God through illness to find new meaning and purpose, and a more developed spirituality. Instead, it can help them to see how God might be speaking to them, to discover how they might respond, and to know the spiritual aspects of their illness. God may be calling them to a new life.

The Old Testament hints that physical health and our connection with God are often related. Such references appear in the story of the exodus, the writings of the prophets, the psalms, and the book of Job. But there is almost no healing in the Old Testament. Jesus' healing work shows the profound relationship between our health and the unfolding of God's purpose in our lives. He takes the basic intuitions of the Old Testament and brings them to fruition.

One Old Testament story shows vividly how listening to our bodies helps us to hear the voice of God. It is the story of Balaam's ass.[10] Balaam was a prophet who lived near the river Jordan. When the people of Israel were moving toward the land of Canaan after the exodus, they came into the land of Moab. The king of Moab, Balak, feared their presence and asked Balaam to curse them. God tells Balaam that these people are blessed and not to be cursed. Balak persists and sends more messengers to Balaam. Finally, Balaam decides to go, but with the intention of doing only what God wills. Balaam gets on his ass and heads for Moab. However, the

ass sees an angel of the Lord standing in front of them on the road holding
a drawn sword. The animal turns off the road into a field. Annoyed,
Balaam strikes it to get it back on the road. Next, they come to a narrow
place with walls on either side—and again the ass sees the angel blocking
their way. The ass pushes up against the wall, pinning Balaam's foot, so he
strikes it again. Then they reach another narrow place, with no room on
either side, and again the angel is there, blocking their way. This time the
ass lies down under Balaam. Balaam gets angry once more and strikes it
with his staff. The text concludes:

> Then the Lord opened the mouth of the ass, and she said to
> Balaam, "What have I done to you, that you have struck me
> three times?" And Balaam said to the ass, "Because you have
> made sport of me. I wish I had a sword in my hand, for then I
> would kill you." And the ass said to Balaam, "Am I not your ass,
> upon which you have ridden all your life long to this day? Was I
> ever accustomed to do so to you?" And he said, "No."
>
> Then the Lord opened the eyes of Balaam, and he saw the
> angel of the Lord standing in the way, with his drawn sword in
> his hand; and he bowed his head, and fell on his face. And the
> angel of the Lord said to him, "Why have you struck your ass
> these three times? Behold, I have come forth to withstand you,
> because your way is perverse before me; and the ass saw me, and
> turned aside before me these three times. If she had not turned
> aside from me, surely just now I would have slain you and let her
> live." Then Balaam said to the angel of the Lord, "I have sinned,
> for I did not know that thou didst stand in the road against me.
> Now therefore, if it is evil in thy sight, I will go back again." And
> the angel of the Lord said to Balaam, "Go with the men; but only
> the word which I bid you, that shall you speak." So Balaam went
> on with the princes of Balak (Num 22:28–35).

Obviously Balaam's ass is no ordinary ass. She talks. She reminds
Balaam that he has ridden her for his entire life. Because of this, the tale is
best seen as describing the inner aspects of Balaam's situation. In shamanistic lore, animals often serve as guiding spirits that aid the shaman in his
life and work. Even today they play an important part in our dreams. The

beast of burden is often synonymous with the body, carrying us through life. Like Balaam's ass, it is with us every day of our life. The story of Balaam's ass can be viewed as a story about the wisdom of the body in perceiving the purposes and presence of God. The body—represented by the ass—sees the divine presence first. When the body takes the ego off its chosen path, the ego reacts by forcing the body back into the direction it wants to go.

The first time Balaam's ass sees the angel, it wanders off the path into a field. This suggest the subtle way the body gives the ego signs that something may not be right with the direction it is heading. Possibly we feel tired, dizzy, or subtly discombobulated. We are taken off the beaten path into a field where we can relax and take stock of our situation. At such moments, we usually react like Balaam and try to keep the body headed right where we want it to go.

The second time Balaam's ass spots the angel, they are walled in on either side. The path is narrow; there is no other place to go. The ass bangs up against one of the walls and Balaam's foot is caught, probably bruised. In symbolic language, injuries to the foot or legs often reflect where we stand in life. At his point Balaam did not have a good standpoint. He did not see the angel up ahead. He did not perceive the divine opposition to the direction he was taking. He suffers a foot injury because the ass, his physical nature, is trying to tell him something. Balaam is only annoyed by the bruise—not moved to examine what he is doing—and once again hits the ass to force it along as he directs.

Finally, Balaam and the ass reach a place so narrow that they can move neither left nor right. Again the ass perceives the angel, and this time it just lies down. This is a marvelous image of the body coming under some debilitating illness—forcing a person to come to a complete stop in life. The ego can no longer keep pushing to move. Now the ego must do some important work. The "narrow place" is an important one.[11] It indicates a life situation the individual must come to terms with. For this passage to be made, the ego must be aligned with the greater wisdom of God. People who reach such points in their lives encounter their unique destiny and personality. Their illness may be a sign of special divine action. The direction they take must be that called for by God, not the ego. Through such an illness (a kind of sit-down strike), the necessary alignment with God's purpose can be carried out.

In the story we hear that the Lord opened the mouth of the ass.

Balaam has no choice but to talk things out with his ass to get to the bottom of them. This dialogue is a good example of what psychology calls active imagination. In active imagination a person takes some figure from a dream, fantasy, or image related to one's pain or illness and begins to talk with that figure.[12] This process involves faith in our internal resources and the power of our imagination, as we saw with the Syrophoenician woman and the woman with a flow of blood. Often, when people first try this form of inner dialogue, they feel "like an ass." Yet such imagination can flow easily as we work at it. Frequently, as in the case of Balaam, it can have a surprising effect.

When Balaam lets the ass speak to him, she asks why he mistreats her—just the sort of question our bodies often ask us. Balaam expresses anger and embarrassment: he feels the ass has made sport of him, made him look bad in the eyes of the princes of Balak. Immediately we discover one of the traps of the ego. Rather than listen to what our bodies tell us, we are concerned with what others think and how we appear to them. We are embarrassed that we cannot function as everyone else does. Balaam is so embarrassed that he would like to do away with his ass altogether. Why do we have to be bothered with our bodies, anyway? They can seem such a nuisance. Yet, as the story indicates, they possess a wisdom greater than we realize. The ass reminds Balaam that she has been there to carry him all these years and never let him down. Likewise, we can easily take our bodies for granted, yet most of the time they do a marvelous job of staying healthy and carrying us through life. But if we take them for granted, it is at our peril: the body may have some very important things to tell us.

When Balaam gets over his embarrassment, listens to the ass, and accepts that the ass has been a faithful friend for all these years, his eyes are opened. He sees the angel. Only when Balaam comes into proper relationship with this bodily side of himself can he see God's messenger and hear his voice. The angel now asks Balaam the same question as the ass: Why did he strike her three times? The angel continues to confront Balaam, pointing out that he stood before Balaam because Balaam's way was not acceptable to him. Had the ass not turned aside, the consequences would have been worse. The ass actually protected Balaam from greater danger. Balaam repents, acknowledges his sin, and offers to go back. The angel tells him that he can go on, but only if he speaks words that the angel shall tell him. As he resumes his journey, Balaam will once again be riding his ass. He will only be able to go this way successfully, however, if he stays in tune with the voice of the angel—an impossibility if he had not first heard the voice of his ass. Listening to the body and the earthy side of life is crucial to the spiritual way. To receive its wisdom is to open our ears to the voice of God.

The symbolism of this story was not lost on the writers of the gospels. As he entered Jerusalem, Jesus sent for a colt to ride.[13] Like Balaam, he fulfills God's purposes by riding an animal symbolic of the instinctual life. The great climax of Jesus' life is lived out in his body. As he rides the colt, he is very aware of his own special way, his unique destiny. He does not ride to receive the adulation of the crowds. He is not acting as others might want, but as God intends. He was to be no different than Balaam and the many people he healed. His way, too, must include his body and his physical nature. Only then would he be completely in tune with the voice of God.

Jesus' suffering and death strongly reinforce the importance of living in the body, difficult as it may be. While during his life Jesus drank with others, the gospels indicate that just before he died he did not partake of any wine to dull the experience. He faced it as completely and consciously as possible.[14] His acceptance of his suffering demonstrated that God's purposes can be found beneath human suffering. He suffered greatly in both body and soul. Along with the physical torment, there was the betrayal by Judas, the desertion of his disciples, Peter's denial, the false trial by the Pharisees, and the death penalty of Pilate. On the cross Jesus became the Archetype of the Invalid, emotionally and physically.

One common notion in Christianity concerning Jesus is that "by his wounds we are healed." Many Christians feel that this traditional theology serves as a guide to God's saving action. Christians assume that the central transformation of Jesus' life can be vicariously applied to their own. The healing work of Jesus and his suffering on the cross remind us that by *our* wounds are we healed. For our wounds, like those of the people healed in the gospels, can lead to new direction and purpose, transformation of both body and soul, and resurrection. Our illnesses can be experiences we enter into much as Jesus entered Jerusalem. They can help us clarify where we need to correct our egocentric attitudes. "Yet not what I will, but what thou wilt," Jesus prayed in Gethsemane (Mk 14:36).[15] His was a painful prayer: wanting not to have this cup passed to him, but accepting it because he knew it to be God's will. Faced with illness or suffering, we are challenged by the gospels to make the same encounter.

Inevitably, Jesus' healing ministry and his suffering on the cross lead us to an encounter with the final "illness"—death. Life, by virtue of our birth, assures each of us this one experience. The gospels present three accounts of the raising of the dead. To complete our review of the healing stories and conclude this examination of the role of illness, it is important next to consider the relationship between healing and death.

NOTES

[1] Parallels found in Mt 8:14–15 and Lk 4:38–39.

[2] C.G. Jung, "Psychology and Religion," *Psychology and Religion: West and East,* p. 11. In the same paragraph, Jung mentions the cure of other physical symptoms through psychological work.

[3] Some schools of psychology, especially the behaviorist school, treat psychological symptoms as something only to be removed, not understood. They approach such symptoms very much as medical doctors approach bodily symptoms. Such an approach ignores the underlying inner situation to which the symptom is trying to point.

[4] See O. Carl Simonton et al., *Getting Well Again.* This book provides a good picture of this side of cancer. (See especially pp. 114–16.) Elida Evans' *A Psychological Study of Cancer* is a very early study demonstrating a relationship between our emotional life and cancer. Bernie Siegel's *Love, Medicine & Miracles* is a more recent book on this subject.

[5] Barbara Coleman, president and founder of the cancer-support group "We Can Do!" has observed that cancer cells, being inferior cells, will herd together. They cannot survive on their own. Cancer patients are often "too good" at conforming to society and are dominated by their own herd instinct. They do not live enough as individuals.

[6] Simonton et al., *Getting Well Again.* Chapter 10, " 'Benefits' of Illness," has some good examples of this.

[7] Adolf Guggenbühl-Craig, "The Archetype of the Invalid and the Limits of Healing."

[8] See John A. Sanford, *Fritz Kunkel: Selected Writings.*

[9] See Cousins, Chapter 4, and Simonton et al., Chapter 16.

[10] Num 22:1–35. A good commentary on this story from the perspective of the meaning of the angel is found in John A. Sanford, *Evil: The Shadow Side of Reality.*

[11] Jesus teaches, "Enter by the narrow gate" (Mt 7:13–14; Lk 13:24). A good commentary on this teaching appears in John A. Sanford, *The Kingdom Within,* pp. 64–66.

[12] See John A. Sanford, *Healing and Wholeness,* Chapter 6: "Healing Ourselves," pp. 140–48, and Albert Kreinheder, "The Healing Power of Illness."

[13] Mark 11:1–10 mentions a colt, as does Luke 19:28–38. Matthew 21:1–9 refers to an ass and a colt, while John 12:12–16 indicates it was an ass' colt.

[14] Mk 14:25; Lk 22:15–18.

[15] Parallels are found in Mt 26:39, Lk 22:42, and Jn 12:27.

Chapter 11
Healing and Death

T he gospel healings challenge us to consider something extraordinary: that healing of the body is possible even in the face of death. Jesus' life makes clear that death is inevitable, and that each of us does well to confront it head-on. Our spiritual life continues after death, and our bodily life can prepare us for it.[1] The shamanistic overview of the healing of Jesus discussed in Chapter 1 is most helpful in understanding the accounts of the raising of the dead and Jesus' approach to death. We begin with the story of Jairus' daughter.

> Then came one of the rulers of the synagogue, Jairus by name; and seeing him, he fell at his feet, and besought him, saying, "My little daughter is at the point of death. Come and lay your hands on her, so that she may be made well, and live." And he went with him. [The story of the healing of the woman with the flow of blood is told here.] While he was still speaking, there came from the ruler's house some who said, "Your daughter is dead. Why trouble the Teacher any further?" But ignoring what they said, Jesus said to the ruler of the synagogue, "Do not fear, only believe." And he allowed no one to follow him except Peter and James and John the brother of James. When they came to the house of the ruler of the synagogue, he saw a tumult, and people weeping and wailing loudly. And when he had entered, he said to them, "Why do you make a tumult and weep? The child is not dead but sleeping." And they laughed at him. But he put them all outside, and took the child's father and mother and those who were with him, and went in where the child was. Taking her by the hand he said to her, "Tal'itha cum'mi"; which means, "Little girl, I say to you, arise." And immediately the girl got up and walked (she was twelve years of age), and they were immediately overcome with amazement. And he strictly charged them that no one should know this, and told them to give her something to eat (Mk 5:22–24a, 35–43).[2]

When Jesus arrived at Jairus' house, he was informed that the girl was already dead. There were no longer any vital signs. But Jesus did not heal from only a physical perspective. He healed like a shaman—from an internal, spiritual one. The shaman is less concerned with the state of the body than with the soul. He ventures into the inner realm to retrieve souls that have become lost in their journey. Thus, as Jesus entered the house and heard that the girl was dead, he sensed that her soul was still close by. He acted to return it to the body. Interestingly, one of the things he does is take her by the hand, giving a living touch to the body presumed to be dead.

All of this may seem strange to western minds, accustomed to perceive illness and death in strictly biological terms. Yet, even in our own day, some patients report being out of their bodies during major surgery and looking down on themselves while the doctors are at work. In many cases this happens when, from a medical viewpoint, the body is dead and has lost all vital signs. When he or she is resuscitated, the person is aware of returning to the body.[3] Such reports are a reminder that much more can be happening in a person who is very ill than the physical difficulty itself. Experiences like these can bring new life and purpose; the young woman chaplain mentioned in the previous chapter, for instance, had an out-of-body experience during an operation that proved to be of profound religious significance for her recovery.

In his autobiography, C.G. Jung reports seeing visions after suffering a heart attack.[4] These visions had an extraordinary beauty for this man already very much at home in the inner world. One of them included being far out in space, and looking back on the earth—like the astronauts many years later. The experiences were so profound that Jung actually resented the efforts of his doctors to keep him alive. Yet when he recovered, he went on to his most creative and profound years, to his most spiritual work. Even though he had wanted to die and merge into the spiritual reality of his visions, something within him pushed him back into bodily life.

A shaman has the unusual capacity to relate to a person in such a state. Most likely, this is how Jesus intervened on behalf of Jairus' daughter. Our story makes clear, however, that there are other important factors at work.

Jairus, the man who came to Jesus, was a synagogue leader, a man in religious authority. Journeying to seek Jesus' help, he takes a great risk: after all, this transient teacher and healer is not accepted by most of his colleagues. When he finds Jesus, he falls at his feet in complete humility. In the face of his daughter's illness, he recognizes his own spiritual helplessness. As we have seen, this was something most of the other religious leaders of the day would not face. This man's love for his daughter broke through all that. Jesus senses his special concern and his willingness to let go of his old religious attitudes. As so often happens when he meets people willing to change, he agrees to help.

This is the only case of a gospel healing story being interrupted by another. Before we find out what happens to this man's daughter, Jesus encounters the woman with the flow of blood.[5] He does not hurry along, even though Jairus has indicated that his daughter is near death. Rather, he recognized death as a completely natural event. This attitude brings to mind the advice of the Yaqui Indian shaman, Don Juan, to an anthropology student who apprenticed with him: one must live as if death was always at one's side.[6] In a similar vein, Jung spoke in his very late years of death being as psychologically important to life as birth.[7] Jesus' approach, then, is the very opposite of that taken by the medical profession in the face of death. There is no special hurry or fear of delay.

Even before they reach Jairus' house, some people come to let them know the bad news. "Your daughter is dead. Why trouble the Teacher any further?" These voices express skepticism about any further efforts on behalf of the daughter. Jesus ignores them and follows through with his original intention, telling Jairus, "Do not fear, only believe." He encourages Jairus and advises him to hold his fear. Death brings out fear in the human soul, but it is a fear, if properly faced, that connects to deeper aspects of ourselves. As we shall see, death is an enemy to the egocentric ego, one that needs to do more work in aligning itself with God. With this fear present, Jesus takes with him only Peter, James, and John—the same three disciples he took onto the mountain for the transfiguration and also into Gethsemane. These experiences were profound shamanistic moments in Jesus' life. The selection of these three disciples for this event at Jairus' home underlies its shamanistic nature.

When they arrive, the people gathered at the house are in turmoil. Jesus questions them. A death has taken place, but he implies that someone with deeper spiritual awareness would disagree. He tells them, "The child is not dead, but sleeping." They laugh at him, thinking he is crazy. The description of the girl as "sleeping" is interesting. For often when we sleep we enter the inner spiritual world through dreams. We are not connected to our bodies in any conscious way, and live primarily in the reality of the soul. Jesus perceived that this was where this girl's soul still resided—really not that far from her body.

When he goes to see the girl, Jesus tries to create the best possible environment. He sends all the others outside, except for the girl's parents and the three disciples: those who are deeply concerned about the child, and those who can best appreciate what he is doing. In this atmosphere he takes the girl by the hand and says, "Little girl, I say to you, arise." She immediately gets up and walks, to the amazement of those present. Her recovery is a perfect example of the return of soul to body in shamanism. Jesus recognized the body's needs at this point, asking the parents to give her something to eat: the body, now once again containing the soul, must be properly cared for. And as he often does with such extraordinary events, Jesus tells those present not to say anything. Such profound spiritual experiences are best carried within, reflected on, and shared only when they can be accepted and understood. The attitude of most people around the house would not be conducive to digesting such experience.

This near-death illness played an important part in this girl's life. Her age and family situation provide helpful clues. As the daughter of a synagogue leader, she was probably raised strictly. We hear at the end of the story that she was twelve, the age of early puberty. Her culture and religion were very patriarchal and did not provide a genuine rite of passage for a young woman. Such rites of passage are far more common in primitive societies.[8] However, if this father fulfilled his role as a conventional religious leader, it would be impossible for him to recognize what was going on in his daughter. When she got as sick as she did, he let go of his customary role and took the risk of seeking out Jesus. His bold action allows him to express his deepest feeling for his daughter and at the same time break out of the spiritual rut his position has imposed on him. We see the same dynamic in our own society, which lacks appropriate rites of initiation for young people. Children and young adults are pushed to find norms they can fill without any attention to their inner development. Part of the problem behind our culture's drug crisis is the lack of recognition of the inner realities that need to come to life in our children as they enter adolescence.

Young people in puberty and adolescence are often faced with a spiritual crisis similar to the one Jung experienced in his sixties. Part of him wished to stay in the world of his visions, but something stronger pulled him back to life. Death probably seemed a viable alternative to Jairus' daughter as she faced growing up in a society that could not help her embrace the realities of her own soul. In our culture, suicide and drugs are often chosen by young people because we lack the rituals to lead them to the full realization of what it is to be an adult man or woman.

The soul of Jairus' daughter was in great crisis. Coming of age as a young woman, she would have to meet numerous social and religious expectations. Yet as her body begins its monthly cycle, her soul is invited to know and experience the deepest mysteries of life. In primitive cultures puberty is a crucial time. The young person is initiated into tribal mysteries and experiences first-hand the spiritual realities known by adults.[9]

There is no fixed time when this occurs for boys, but with girls it always takes place at the first period. The spiritual mysteries of young men and women are different. The young man's is symbolized by the erect penis. He is moved to penetrate more into life, to make a mark for himself in the world. The young woman's is reflected in the flow of her menstrual blood. She becomes attuned to new emotional rhythms and the capacity to create life from within herself. In the patriarchal society of Jesus' time, feminine spiritual mysteries were lost. The woman with a flow of blood, who approached Jesus while he was going to Jairus' home, had to search many years to find healing. Her recovery depended on reconnecting to the feminine spiritual life within herself. Only Jesus, attuned to the spiritual depths men and women share, could assist her.

Menstruation is deeply related to the mysteries of the feminine soul. After the other woman encounters her inner images and returns to her natural menstrual cycle, Jairus' daughter experiences these mysteries in a way not available through her father and the other religious leaders. She becomes aware of this spiritual reality and its power to transform when Jesus perceives her young soul's dilemma. Her healing is an experience of death and rebirth that paves the way for her adult life.

Lately, in our own patriarchal society, women are recognizing their spiritual loss and beginning to discover ways to fill the void. Feminism has moved beyond social and economic difficulties to seek healing for spiritual wounds as well.[10] Women's psychological and spiritual health is intimately connected to their bodily life.[11] Jesus knew this relationship very well.

More than an extraordinary story, the healing of Jairus' daughter points to aspects of life that we no longer attend to. Jairus was lucky. His feelings for his daughter led him to the right man at the right moment. While we are not likely to find a healer such as Jesus today, there are resources for those, like Jairus, who are moved to search for them. We can seek healing in many forms, both for ourselves and for others. It should not stop even if death seems imminent. The qualities that help a person find his way through life are equally important in making the passage through death.

This story is the most authentic of the three gospel accounts of the raising of the dead. It can be understood from the viewpoint of shamanism, and it appears in all three synoptic gospels. The other two stories are the raising of the widow's son at Nain, found only in Luke, and the raising of Lazarus, found only in John. Here is the story from Luke:

> Soon afterward he went to a city called Nain, and his disciples and a great crowd went with him. As he drew near to the gate of the city, behold, a man who had died was being carried out, the only son of his mother, and she was a widow; and a large crowd from the city was with her. And when the Lord saw her, he had compassion on her and said to her, "Do not weep." And he came and touched the bier, and the bearers stood still. And he said, "Young man, I say to you, arise." And the dead man sat up, and began to speak. And he gave him to his mother. Fear seized them all; and they glorified God, saying, "A great prophet has arisen among us!" and "God has visited his people!" And this report concerning him spread through the whole of Judea and all the surrounding country (Lk 7:11–17).

This story parallels the Old Testament account of the healing of the widow's son by the prophet Elijah, itself a rare example of shamanistic healing in Israelite history.[12] Elijah came very close to shamanism. Praying for healing for the boy, he asks, "O Lord my God, let this child's soul come into him again." Then we are told, "And the Lord harkened to the voice of Elijah; and the soul of the child came into him again"—an excellent description of shamanistic healing. At the end of the story the woman declares that now she knows that Elijah is a man of God and that the words he speaks are true.

Luke tells this parallel story to compare Jesus and Elijah. From what we have seen of Jesus' healing, he was certainly justified in doing so. The declaration by the people at the end of the gospel story parallels the woman's declaration to Elijah after he had healed her son. Luke includes a passage in which Jesus indicates to the disciples of John the Baptist that they can know that God is present in his ministry because of the healing that takes place. God is present in Jesus' ministry just as he was present in Old Testament times.

With this story Luke not only reiterates the importance of Jesus' healing ministry, but emphasizes other themes significant to him. Of the four evangelists, Luke is the most concerned with widows, the poor, and the downtrodden.[13] By telling this story, he indicates to his readers that such concerns also mattered to Jesus. Luke tells us that when Jesus saw the widow he had compassion on her.[14] He felt that such compassion should be evident in Christian life, and should lead to a caring attitude toward society's outcasts.

If this healing actually took place, it is hard to imagine why none of the other evangelists mentions it. Possibly Luke built his story around some healing that did not come to their attention. We have seen Luke's tendency to carry the facts of Jesus' healings further than the other synoptic evangelists, in order to help emphasize points important to his gospel. Whether this healing actually took place, it amplifies important aspects of Jesus' healing.

John also tells a story that does not appear in any of the other three gospels:

> Now a certain man was ill, Lazarus of Bethany, the village of Mary and her sister Martha. It was Mary who anointed the Lord with ointment and wiped his feet with her hair, whose brother Lazarus was ill. So the sisters sent to him, saying, "Lord, he whom you love is ill." But when Jesus heard it he said, "This illness is not unto death; it is for the glory of God, so that the Son of God may be glorified by means of it."
>
> Now Jesus loved Martha and her sister and Lazarus. So when he heard that he was ill, he stayed two days longer in the place where he was. Then after this he said to his disciples, "Let us go into Judea again." The disciples said to him, "Rabbi, the Jews were but now seeking to stone you, and are you going there again?" Jesus answered, "Are there not twelve hours in the day? If any one walks in the day, he does not stumble, because he sees the light of this world. But if anyone walks in the night, he stumbles, because the light is not in him." Thus he spoke, and then he said to them, "Our friend Lazarus has fallen asleep, but I go to awake him out of sleep." The disciples said to him, "Lord, if he has fallen asleep, he will recover." Now Jesus had spoken of his death, but they thought that he meant taking rest in sleep. Then Jesus told them plainly, "Lazarus is dead; and for your sake I am glad that I was not there, so that you may believe. But let us

go to him." Thomas, called the Twin, said to his fellow disciples, "Let us also go, that we may die with him."

Now when Jesus came, he found that Lazarus had already been in the tomb four days. Bethany was near Jerusalem, about two miles off, and many of the Jews had come to Martha and Mary to console them concerning their brother. When Martha heard that Jesus was coming, she went and met him, while Mary sat in the house. Martha said to Jesus, "Lord, if you had been here, my brother would not have died. And even now I know that whatever you ask from God, God will give you." Jesus said to her, "Your brother will rise again." Martha said to him, "I know that he will rise again in the resurrection at the last day." Jesus said to her, "I am the resurrection and the life; he who believes in me, though he die, yet shall he live, and whoever lives and believes in me shall never die. Do you believe this?" She said to him, "Yes, Lord; I believe that you are the Christ, the Son of God, he who is coming into the world."

When she had said this, she went and called her sister Mary, saying quietly, "The teacher is here and is calling for you." And when she heard it, she rose quickly and went to him. Now Jesus had not yet come to the village, but was still in the place where Martha had met him. When the Jews who were with her in the house, consoling her, saw Mary rise quickly and go out, they followed her, supposing that she was going to the tomb to weep there. Then Mary, when she came where Jesus was and saw him, fell at his feet, saying to him, "Lord, if you had been here, my brother would not have died." When Jesus saw her weeping, and the Jews who came with her also weeping, he was deeply moved in spirit and troubled; and he said, "Where have you laid him?" They said to him, "Lord, come and see." Jesus wept. So the Jews said, "See how he loved him!" But some of them said, "Could not he who opened the eyes of the blind man have kept this man from dying?"

Then Jesus, deeply moved again, came to the tomb; it was a cave, and a stone lay upon it. Jesus said, "Take away the stone." Martha, the sister of the dead man, said to him, "Lord, by this time there will be an odor, for he has been dead four days." Jesus said to her, "Did I not tell you that if you would believe you would see the glory of God?" So they took away the stone. And

Jesus lifted up his eyes and said, "Father, I thank thee that thou
hast heard me. I knew that thou hearest me always, but I have
said this on account of the people standing by, that they may
believe that thou didst send me." When he had said this, he cried
with a loud voice, "Lazarus, come out." The dead man came out,
his hands and feet bound with bandages, and his face wrapped
with a cloth. Jesus said to them, "Unbind him, and let him go"
(Jn 11:1–44).

Did this story actually happen? Probably not as it is told. Nevertheless,
like any good story, it teaches us a great deal. In many ways it is a bridge
between accounts like the healing of Jairus' daughter and Jesus' own resurrection. It is the most dramatic transformation outside of the resurrection.
This story describes characters—Lazarus, Martha, and Mary—mentioned
only in the two later gospels. If such a dramatic story actually took place, it
is hard to believe that Mark, Matthew, and Luke would make no mention
of it.

Lazarus, whom Jesus loves, is ill—not just anyone, but someone Jesus
personally cares for and already knows. He announces that this illness is
not unto death, thereby setting the stage for a lesson on mortality. The
evangelist says that Jesus loved Lazarus and his two sisters, adding that
when Jesus heard Lazarus was ill he stayed two days longer in the place
where he was. Do we take in the impact of this? Jesus waited *two days*
before he left to assist a man he reportedly loved. This is the theme of
waiting we have seen in connection with the healing of Jairus' daughter.
There, Jesus allowed himself to be interrupted for the sake of healing. Here
he waits on purpose. As he does so often, John amplifies principles expressed in the other gospels. As we have seen, spiritual problems and
difficulties cannot be approached in haste.

When Jesus is finally ready to go, his disciples are surprised. The
Jewish leaders are out to stone him. He goes to Lazarus in the face of his
own death. Jesus talks about walking in the day and being able to see the
light of the world, and walking at night and stumbling because the light is
not there. These words refer to the importance of consciousness, not only
for healing as we discussed in Chapter 6, but also in the face of death. Jesus
makes this journey conscious both of the threat from the Jewish leaders
and of what God wants him to do.

The disciples are unconscious of what is going on, especially with
regard to Lazarus. Their perceptions are paralyzed by the threat of death

they feel as companions of Jesus. Jesus announces that Lazarus has fallen asleep—the same phrase he used about Jairus' daughter before her heal- ing. The disciples take this literally and assume that Lazarus will get well. Jesus then tells them in a straightforward way that Lazarus is dead. Here we see how John develops his stories beyond the originals found in Mark. John not only reports a healing but provides an important discourse about confronting death. When Jesus informs the disciples directly that Lazarus is dead, he invites them to go with him, risking their lives. In doing so, the disciples move a little closer to coming to terms with their own fears.

When Jesus arrives in Bethany, Lazarus had been in the tomb four days. John wants to go beyond Luke's story showing Jesus healing like Elijah. The mention of four days makes it definite that Lazarus is dead. This is confirmed when Martha warns Jesus about the odor of the body as he approaches the tomb. John goes so far as to indicate that the corpse has started to decay. This is more than just a story of shamanistic revival of the body. It is a discourse on meeting the stench of death and its horrible reality.

In the next passage, John presents some of his own theology. To him, the way of Jesus is a way of life, even in the face of death. Approached properly, death can be an introduction to a new level of consciousness. At the same time, this part of the story shows the human response to death—the loss of a person one has loved and compassion for those who mourn. Both Martha and Mary would have liked for their brother to live, and they believe that Jesus could have saved him. Even as they speak with him in terms of resurrection, there is disappointment and anger at his delay. Then there are the grief and tears, not only of the sisters, but of those with them. These realities, spiritual and emotional, must come to- gether. Jesus shares both. Even as he moves toward the tomb, aware of what God will do through him, he experiences the sorrow of losing his friend. Spiritual transformation and human emotion cannot be separated. Both are vital to shamanistic spirituality. Together they bring healing and solace, whether to a soul that will still go forward in this life or to one about to be transformed as part of its journey to the world beyond.

Lazarus, wrapped head to toe and lying in a tomb, epitomizes the condition of one who is spiritually dead and bound. Healing, whether in the face of death or of illness, releases the soul from its bonds and sets it free. The more a soul develops in spiritual awareness, the smaller the threat of death. Death is life's last great challenge to the ego to free the soul, to let it be guided by the spirit or inner voice of God. Many people continue to deny the reality of death or play intellectual games with it, a real problem in our society. Fortunately, some professionals are developing a new aware-ness of the need to come to terms with death in a healthy way so that we can live life more fully.[15]

Death raises many questions about life, more than one chapter can answer. Others, whose books are cited in the notes, have written more on this topic. One aspect I would like to pursue is that death confronts us with the ultimate meaning and purpose of our lives. It forces us to examine our relationship with the eternal. Death holds out final opportunities for growth, self-awareness, and spiritual consciousness, by no means guaran-teeing them, but offering them to those who approach with the best atti-tude. Of course, waiting until death is imminent to find one's way and to develop a personal and spiritual consciousness is foolhardy. The sooner one begins such a quest, the more likely one will be prepared for death and what comes after. One is also in a much better position to assist others who are confronting death.

A good example is provided by the story of Craig, an eight year old cancer patient. He and his family wrestled with his illness for a number of years. Such an illness in a young child in our culture is very tragic, since the majority of children live to adulthood. This was not always so, and until relatively recently many families were all too familiar with the reality of early death. Perhaps the most significant contribution of modern medical science is the decrease in the mortality rate of our children. Unfortunately, this only makes the death of a child like Craig seem all the more tragic.

Remarkably, a child like Craig often handles the situation better than anyone. Adults have the most difficulty. The night of Craig's death his grandmother, echoing the feelings of many, remarked how much he had taught those who came to know him. As he approached death, he seemed older than his years. Just before he died, he was in pain, and it was sug-gested that he try to meditate using some techniques that he had learned earlier. This time he could not imagine himself on the beach at one of his favorite places. Trying only made him sad because he knew he was not there. His father suggested he make another attempt. This time Craig imagined himself sitting on the lap of Jesus in front of a tree full of green leaves:

> *They are sitting on a rock and it is all brown around them. The sky is pink. It is starting to get dark. There is a pond on the other side of the tree. In the pond are some frogs, tadpoles, and three goldfish. God wanted to make them pretty to look at.*

There is a bluebird near them. Pretty soon a beaver comes down to the pond. It is getting lighter again. There is moss around the tree. Instead of sitting on the rock, Jesus and Craig are sitting on the soft green moss. Mary and Joseph and God bring them a picnic lunch. There are lots of good fruits—cantaloupes, apples and oranges—and water. Jesus turns the water into wine, just as happens at church. Jesus is talking to him now, telling him about all the miracles he has done for him.[16]

Craig's meditation was filled with his favorite things. It offered him and his family a beautiful image of intimacy with God. Now Craig could enter his final hours at peace and without fear. The effect carried over to the others. Everyone felt good about this meditation. Children like Craig are far more capable of using their imaginations in this way than most adults. They are closer to the resources of the soul. We can learn from them how to react spontaneously and imaginatively in life even when confronted with death.

Jung reports an extraordinary set of dreams presented by a ten year old girl to her father.[17] The father, a psychiatrist, did not know what to make of them. They had no link to his daughter's personal experience. Still, Jung points out, all the dreams had important archetypal patterns, with both Christian and non-Christian themes. The girl had not done any study that could account for their appearance. A year later, she died of an infectious disease. Jung indicates that her dreams combined themes for the initiation of young people usually found in primitive cultures with themes that were a preparation for death and the deeper mysteries of life.

Jung lists twelve motifs from the dreams. The first motif is: " 'The evil animal,' a snakelike monster with many horns, kills and devours all other animals. But God comes from the four corners, being in fact four separate gods, and gives rebirth to all the dead animals." This motif expresses both Christian and primitive themes. Christian restitution is expressed in a manner similar to the apocalyptic literature of the early church. Such images are also commonly found in primitive mythology, especially in the initiation ceremonies of early adolescence.

The fifth motif is also noteworthy: "A drop of water is seen as it appears when looked at through a microscope. The girl sees that the drop is full of tree branches. This portrays the origin of the world." This image juxtaposes a modern scientific instrument with ideas from ancient cosmologies. The whole is discovered by examining a part. Jungian analysis works much like this. As the reality of an individual is explored, the whole of the cosmos or archetypal world opens up. The depiction of the origin of the world was common in the primitive initiation of young people. The young girl who dreamed these motifs approached puberty, much like Jairus' daughter.

The last of the dream motifs was: "Swarms of gnats obscure the sun, the moon, and all the stars, except one. That one star falls upon the dreamer." Many ancient people believed that a star was born in the sky at each person's birth. This dream image reflects the girl's impending death. Her life was cut short, but inwardly she experienced a fullness of life's mysteries that few people allow into their consciousness. Like Craig, she did not leave this earthly life without some experience of inner spiritual treasures.

From a strictly physical perspective, death is the enemy of healing. To shamans it is life's final call to encounter the numinous, spiritual world. This world is as close as our dreams; we can relate to it at any time. The shamanistic view of healing and death calls each of us to take spiritual reality to heart all through life. We can postpone it, but not avoid it.

Before leaving this topic, it is worth noting that the Pharisees believed in angels, spirits, and the resurrection of the dead. Jesus' struggles with them point up that mere *belief* in spiritual things will not bring healing. How one *lives* is far more important. The legalism of the Pharisees got in the way of healing and prevented them from experiencing the inner dimensions of the personality. As we have seen, this attitude contributed to much of the illness Jesus had to deal with. The same conflict exists in dealing with death. A belief in life after death will not prepare one for death, just as it will not equip one to heal. True spiritual consciousness is necessary for developing healing and facing death, more than specific beliefs.

NOTES

[1] See Morton T. Kelsey, *Afterlife: The Other Side of Dying,* for a good presentation on the importance of a sense of an afterlife in day-to-day living.

[2] Parallels are found in Mt 9:18–19, 23–26, and Lk 8:41–42a, 49–56.

[3] See Raymond Moody, Jr., M.D., *Life After Life,* and *Reflections on Life After Life.*

[4] See C.G. Jung, *Memories, Dreams, Reflections,* Chapter 10, "Visions," and Chapter 11, "On Life After Death."

[5] See Chapter 8.

[6] Carlos Casteneda, *The Teachings of Don Juan: A Yaqui Way of Knowledge.*

[7] "Face to Face," BBC interview of Jung with John Freeman.

[8] For example, the Sioux Indians have a special rite for the coming of age of a young woman. See Marla N. Power, "Menstruation and Reproduction: An Oglala Case."

[9] Mircea Eliade, *Rites and Symbols of Initiation: The Mysteries of Birth and Rebirth.* See also Louise Carus Mahdi, Steven Foster & Meredith Little, *Betwixt & Between: Patterns of Masculine and Feminine Initiation.*

[10] Naomi R. Goldenberg, *Changing of the Gods: Feminism and the End of Traditional Religions.* Jean Shinoda Bolen, *Goddesses in Everywoman: A New Psychology of Women.* Carol P. Christ and Judith Plaskow, *Womanspirit Rising: A Feminist Reader in Religion.*

[11] For example, see Marion Woodman's *The Owl Was a Baker's Daughter: Obesity, Anorexia Nervosa, and the Repressed Feminine,* and *Addiction to Perfection: The Still Unravished Bride.*

[12] 1 Kgs 17:17–24.

[13] Matthew and John make no mention of widows. Mark mentions them only twice (Mk 12.40 and 12:42–43). Luke refers to them six times in his gospel (Lk 2:37, 4:25–26, 7:12, 18:3–5, 20:47, and 21:2–3) and three more in Acts (Acts 6:1, 9:39, and 9:10).

[14] Luke uses the Greek word *splag.hnistheis* discussed in Chapter 4.

[15] Elisabeth Kübler-Ross is recognized as pioneering this work in our country. See her *On Death and Dying* and *Death: The Final Stage of Growth.* Jane Hollister Wheelright's *The Death of a Woman* and Mark Pelgrin's *And a Time to Die* are well-documented accounts of individuals consciously struggling with life while approaching death.

[16] My appreciation to Jim and Pat Schlanser of Pasadena, California, for sharing this material. After Craig's death the Schlansers began a chapter of the Candlelighter Program, which offers support to parents of children with life-threatening diseases.

[17] C.G. Jung, *Man and His Symbols,* pp. 69f.

Chapter 12
The Call to Healing

It is tempting for Christians to marvel at the gospel healing stories, celebrate what Jesus was able to do, and sit back feeling good that all has been taken care of. Unfortunately, this leads to Christian Pharisaism and neglects one of Jesus' primary intentions—having his disciples carry on the *same* healing work. The book of Acts makes clear that the first disciples continued some healing, but it never took as important a place in the life of Christianity as it did for Jesus. While healing has never totally disappeared from the practice of the church,[1] it has never again flourished as it did in the gospels. Part of the reason has to do with the later evangelists. By elaborating their healing stories to paint a picture of Jesus as more divine, they unwittingly led their readers away from the original dynamics of Jesus' healing. Belief in Jesus became more important than carrying on his life and work.

According to the gospels, the core of Jesus' life consisted of two things: proclaiming the kingdom of God[2] and healing. Both contain similar psychological and spiritual themes. Proclaiming God's kingdom brings it closer to others, and this means healing. Healing others as Jesus did requires knowledge of the inner spiritual realities and the capacity to mediate them to others. Matthew makes this clear, describing the life of Jesus in capsule form: "And he went about all Galilee, teaching in their synagogues and preaching the gospel of the kingdom and healing every disease and every infirmity among the people" (Mt 4:23).[3]

Both Matthew and Luke tell of John the Baptist sending his disciples to find out if Jesus is the one they expect to come or if they should expect another. Jesus points to the fruits of his work. "Go and tell John what you hear and see: the blind receive their sight and the lame walk, lepers are cleansed and the deaf hear, and the dead are raised up, and the poor have good news preached to them" (Mt 11:4–5).[4] Healing and proclaiming the good news are signs for Jesus of the presence of God in himself or anyone else.

A passage in John emphasizes what mattered most to Jesus: not faith in himself, but faith in his accomplishments. "If I am not doing the works of my Father, then do not believe me; but if I do them, even though you do not believe me, believe the works, that you may know and understand that the Father is in me and I am in the Father" (Jn 10:37–38). Jesus directs this comment to those who would do away with him. He does not try to save himself. He hopes to alert all he meets to the reality of healing and give them a taste of God's living presence.

Jesus made his teachings and healing available to any who were open, interested, and had the proper attitude. Many responded, not only the disciples. He saw potential in his followers for the same healing that he had offered in his own life. "And Jesus went about all the cities and villages, teaching in their synagogues and preaching the gospel of the kingdom, and healing every disease and every infirmity. When he saw the crowds, he had compassion for them, because they were harassed and helpless, like sheep without a shepherd. Then he said to his disciples, 'The harvest is plentiful, but the laborers are few; pray therefore the Lord of the harvest to send out laborers into his harvest' " (Mt 9:35–38).[5] The harvest, of course, is those people open to the reality of the kingdom of heaven and transformation. The laborers were those who could mediate the kingdom and healing. Many laborers were required. It was not Jesus' work alone; his disciples share and carry out this work.

However, the disciples had limited success. In Mark, Jesus sends the twelve out two by two and gives them authority over unclean spirits. They go out, cast out demons, and heal the sick (Mk 6:7, 13).[6] But they cannot heal the deaf and dumb boy, and Jesus must intervene.[7] They need further growth and development. Their inability to assist this boy and his father frustrates Jesus. Much work is to be done and he cannot do it alone. Mark's gospel reflects this situation—the disciples learn about the spiritual life and healing, but not as well as Jesus had hoped. They could not reach the depth in their healing work that Jesus did.

Likewise, Matthew tells us that Jesus sent out the twelve with authority over unclean spirits and to heal (Mt 10:1). More specifically he charges them, "And preach as you go, saying, 'The kingdom of heaven is at hand.' Heal the sick, raise the dead, cleanse lepers, cast out demons" (Mt 10:7–8a). Much the same commission is found in Luke: "And he called the twelve together and gave them power and authority over all demons and to cure diseases, and he sent them out to preach the kingdom of God and to heal" (Lk 9:1–2). Luke relates that the disciples healed as they went about preaching the kingdom. Jesus is commissioning the disciples for the work he was doing. He does not send them out to preach about *him,* but about the kingdom he himself preaches. Along with preaching comes the work of healing. Luke extends the commissioning of the disciples even further than Mark or Matthew, adding a commissioning of seventy other disciples (Lk 10:1f). Jesus tells them, "Heal the sick in it [the town they enter] and say to them, 'The kingdom of God has come near to you.' " Luke stresses that everyone who follows in Jesus' footsteps must carry on his work.

Finally, John reiterates the importance of Jesus' work being shared. In the story of the man born blind, Jesus tells his disciples that "*we* must work the works of him who sent me" (Jn 9:4, italics mine). Later he adds, "Truly, truly, I say to you, he who believes in me will also do the works that I do; and greater works than these will he do, because I go to the Father" (Jn 14:12). John goes further than the other evangelists; he says that because of Jesus' death and resurrection we should not only be able to duplicate his work of healing and proclaiming the kingdom, but do even better! Through the resurrection, John believes this work can be extended even further than while Jesus lived.

And yet, Christianity has never embraced healing with Jesus' original fervor. It is clear from the gospels that Jesus' followers were meant to continue his work: "These things I have spoken to you, while I am still with you. But the counselor, the Holy Spirit, whom the Father will send in my name, he will teach you things, and bring to your remembrance all that I have said to you" (Jn 14:25–26). John believes that the Holy Spirit will teach us as much as Jesus himself and bring alive all that he left for us. "And I will pray the Father, and he will give you another counselor, to be with you for ever, even the Spirit of truth, whom the world cannot receive, because it neither sees him nor knows him; you know him, for he dwells with you, and will be in you" (Jn 14:16–17). From this counselor will come our continued knowledge of God's will, and we must find it within ourselves. The church claims to have heard its voice since its earliest days and to speak of its work and presence. But if hearing this voice means practicing the healing work as described in the gospels, then the Spirit is not truly being heard. Our inner lives may be far deeper, richer, and more frightening than Christianity has generally allowed us to experience.

John claims that it is better for Jesus not to be with us if we are to learn all that God intends about healing. The early disciples could not attain his level of healing. The implication is that they had to be on their own to discover the spirit within themselves. "Nevertheless I tell you the truth: it is to your advantage that I go away, for if I do not go away, the counselor will not come to you; but if I go, I will send him to you" (Jn 16:7). To complete their spiritual development, the disciples had to hear the voice of God themselves.

According to John, Jesus departed this world having accomplished God's work and aware that those left behind had an equally important work. "And now I am no more in the world, but they are in the world, and I am coming to thee. Holy Father, keep them in thy name, which thou hast given me, that they may be one, even as we are one" (Jn 17:11). What does this mean? Oneness has to do with being complete or whole. A striving for oneness is also a striving for health in the fullest sense, a harmonious linking of body and soul.[8] Through the pursuit of oneness or wholeness we seek our God-given way. Jesus became whole, John tells us, as he neared the completion of his life and fulfilled the purposes God intended for him. The Spirit of God seeks to bring all human beings to oneness.

If God is oneness, and the Holy Spirit, the counselor, lies within each of us to lead us on our journey to become whole, then the Christian church should ask where it is not whole. What aspects of life does it leave out? As it discovers areas in which it does not reflect the oneness of God, it can begin to restore the healing work of Jesus. His life suggests healing as a barometer or yardstick of the life of Christianity.

The faith of the early church is primarily set forth in the life and letters of Paul and the other New Testament epistles. There are two significant differences between these documents and the gospels. First, we look at a shift in the focus of faith.

Günther Bornkamm, an eminent New Testament scholar, at the conclusion of his excellent book *Jesus of Nazareth,* makes an important observation.[9] While Jesus lived, he devoted his life to proclaiming the kingdom of God. The early church, especially in Paul, set about proclaiming Jesus. This was a dramatic shift. As Bornkamm states, the early church ended up proclaiming the proclaimer, rather than the kingdom. We can understand their enthusiasm, but such a proclamation ran counter to Jesus' own purpose. Preaching the kingdom of God and healing, the two things Jesus did the most in his life and set out for his disciples to do, were forgotten. Even within the gospels, the healing stories became altered with time by the growing urge of the evangelists to expand their portrait of Jesus. The increasingly expanded proclamation about Jesus colored more and more the healing art he was trying to pass on to his disciples.

Study of the New Testament shows that important aspects of Jesus' teachings were changed from the very beginning. As one clergyman has put it, we actually have a religion *about* Jesus rather than the religion *of* Jesus.[10] The religious life of Jesus was filled with healing, a sense that the Paraclete, the Holy Spirit, can work within each of us.

The second important difference between the gospels and the rest of the New Testament is in the level of psychology found in each. As John A. Sanford has pointed out in *The Kingdom Within,* the teachings of Jesus have tremendous psychological significance, especially from an inner point of view. We have also seen that the gospel healing stories involve many important psychological dynamics. Much more takes place than simple miraculous intervention. The psychological themes in these stories parallel those of Jesus' teachings. Paul and the other New Testament authors do not exhibit comparable psychological awareness. A high level of consciousness was needed for such healing and preaching. One of the primary reasons for change in the early life of Christianity was the loss of the psychological awareness that Jesus displayed.

During the twenty centuries since, there have been many Christians of profound psychological insight. But the healing life of the church has lacked the foundation of a viable psychology. This unfortunate situation may change with the advent of modern depth psychology, for it will take a psychology capable of showing us the whole to restore a true emphasis on Jesus' healing.

Jung wrote that the challenge for modern Christianity is to affect the soul.[11] Through the centuries the church has been too externally oriented, making dogma and ritual the predominant focus. Depth psychology challenges Christianity to recognize the reality of the psyche so that once again the church can take up its appointed task of making people well. Until the church responds to the needs of the individual soul, its vitality will continue to be sapped. Jesus showed how the soul and body can be powerfully healed and transformed. The future of Christianity (and the world) hinges on whether his followers can become the agents of similar transformations.

One crucial element in this process involves recognizing what has been called the problem of the shadow. Sanford discusses this phenomenon at length.[12] The shadow is the unlived, rejected, despised side of a person's personality, the side that contradicts the ego's ideal. For example, in the story of the man with the withered hand, Jesus makes the Pharisees conscious of their shadows. They are plotting against him as a breaker of sacred religious laws, and yet by doing so are actually breaking these laws in their own hearts.[13] We have seen how they project their shadow—that which contradicted their rigid codes—onto Jesus. This unconscious split between their religious ideals and the reality of their hearts created the environment that makes the man ill. When he understands this problem, he finds healing.

Sanford points out that Jesus was very aware of the reality of the shadow and the need to integrate it within oneself. Paul, a former Pharisee, never succeeded in resolving this split. He saw the tension from this inner struggle, but did not realize that the more he developed his one-sided standards for Christian life and behavior, the worse this problem became. The best example is found in Galatians 5:12, where Paul argues that non-Jews who become Christians need not be circumcised. In his enthusiasm, he suggests that the knife slip on those who insist on this practice and they castrate themselves.[14] This is Paul's shadow—going completely against the attitude he espouses for others. For all his insight and devotion, Paul was not very far along in this important area of the soul. It affected not only his ministry, but that of his followers. His teaching created the same spiritual and psychological trap for others that the Pharisees had set for the man with the withered hand.

Those of us whose ideals are built on traditional religious values like to disclaim the shadow. It cannot be part of ourselves. We either deny it, and so encourage it to erupt in psychological or physical symptoms, or project it onto others. Whole races can project their shadows onto other races as a rationale for their persecution and even destruction. The treatment of Jews by the Germans during World War II is a classic example, but so is our handling in this country of blacks, native Americans, and other ethnic minorities. These people embody aspects of humanity we would rather not see or accept in ourselves. The Pharisees did this with Jesus, and opposing Christian figures have done this with each other through the ages. To the ego, the shadow is evil and counter to the purposes of God.

In fact, the reverse is the case. The shadow is part of our uniqueness, necessary for personal development and healing. Evil works to shore up the ego's own view and prevents integration of the shadow. Recognizing this side of our personality connects us more solidly to the voice of God. Rejecting the shadow can lead to ill health and inhuman treatment of others, even in the name of God. Accepting and integrating the shadow can lead to fuller and richer life and add an important dimension to healing.

In the gospel of John Jesus prays to the Father on behalf of his disciples, "I do not pray that thou shouldst take them out of the world, but that thou shouldst keep them from the evil one" (Jn 17:15). The spiritual way is not an escape from life, nor is life itself evil. The instincts that so frightened Paul are a part of life and need to be integrated into our personalities. The danger is in the attitude we take toward them. Evil works by inflating the ego and making it feel superior to whatever might challenge it to become more whole and conscious. Jesus never rejects anyone, even those the Pharisees consider the most miserable of sinners. The work of the evil one is seen in the attitudes of the Pharisees, active to the detriment of the whole personality and to the healing process.

This approach is summarized in a passage in Luke:

> He also told them a parable: "Can a blind man lead a blind man? Will they not both fall into a pit? A disciple is not above his teacher, but every one when he is fully taught will be like his teacher. Why do you see the speck that is in your brother's eye, but do not notice the log that is in your own eye? Or how can you say to your brother, 'Brother, let me take out the speck that is in your eye,' when you yourself do not see the log that is in your own eye? You hypocrite, first take the log out of your own eye, and then you will see clearly to take out the speck that is in your brother's eye" (Lk 6:39–42).

As we saw in Chapter 6, blindness in the gospels refers primarily to a spiritual condition. Spiritual sight (or consciousness) is essential if we are not to get stuck along the way. The conscious disciple will be most like his teacher. The fully developed Christian disciple will resemble Jesus in the work that he does. The undeveloped disciple will be caught in the tempta-tion to set himself above the rest of life in a way that leads to self-impor-tance. Undeveloped Christians similarly feel they are special in God's eye. Like the Pharisees, they become caught in a dangerous and unconscious shadow problem in which they reject vital aspects of their own personali-ties and of life in general. They do not see with honest spiritual sight, for their vision is clouded by the log in their own eye. Their distorted spiritual consciousness allows them to see only the speck in their neighbor's eye—the person or persons around them onto whom they project their own shadow.

Jesus' parable reveals that the primary stumbling block to clear-sighted vision is not in those around us, but in ourselves. The log that affects our own vision requires much greater attention than the speck we see in our neighbor. The significance for healing is clear. True healing begins with ourselves and those things that cloud our own vision of life. We must come to terms with our shadow. As we do, we respond to Jesus' call to heal and to live fully. In *Power in the Helping Professions,* Adolf Guggenbühl-Craig warns that those in the position of helping others—doctors, psychotherapists, clergy, nurses, social workers, and the like—must be particularly attuned to the shadow problem so that they do not unconsciously inflict it on those they are trying to help. Theirs can be the biggest log of all. The same applies to every Christian who hears God's call to be an agent of healing.

Luke follows this parable with a passage about the tree that bears good fruit and the tree that bears bad fruit (Lk 6:43–45). The goodness is determined not by outer actions or monuments we might build for ourselves, but by our inner condition. The good man produces good fruit out of the treasure of his heart. As we have seen, "heart" is synonymous with the inner self or unconscious. The good man has wrestled with his shadow. He acknowledges his complete personality—his capacity for doing evil as well as good. He can then truly bear good fruit. On the other hand, the evil man has an evil treasure in his heart. He has pushed down his shadow and not brought it up to the light of consciousness where it can be accepted and integrated. Left in the unconscious, the shadow gains its negative reputation. It turns dark because it has been rejected by the ego and thus manifests itself at inappropriate times and in unpleasant ways as "bad fruit."

No one has completely resolved his inner situation, of course. However, careful attention to this difficult area can help us find God's way. As we work on the log in our own eye, we will see more clearly to assist others. To ignore or deny the shadow invites evil of a worse kind, the same evil that brought on the suffering and death of Jesus.

Finally, Luke distinguishes between listening to Jesus' words and merely making some kind of personal proclamation about him.

> "Why do you call me 'Lord, Lord,' and not do what I tell you?
> Every one who comes to me and hears my words and does them,
> I will show you what he is like: he is like a man building a house,
> who dug deep, and laid the foundation upon rock; and when a
> flood arose, the stream broke against that house, and could not
> shake it, because it had been well built. But he who hears and
> does not do them is like a man who built a house on the ground
> without a foundation, against which the stream broke, and im-
> mediately it fell, and the ruin of that house was great" (Lk
> 6:46–49).

If we are going to continue the healing work begun by Jesus, we must also do the psychological work necessary to build a proper foundation.

NOTES

[1] See Morton T. Kelsey, *Christianity and Healing.*

[2] See John A. Sanford, *The Kingdom Within.*

[3] As we have seen, Matthew and Luke tend to overstate the specifics of Jesus' healing. Nevertheless, they reflect the key elements of his life accurately. See also Lk 9:11.

[4] See also Lk 7:22.

[5] See also Lk 8:1 and 10:2.

[6] The reference in Mark 6:13 to the use of oil in the healing work of the disciples probably reflects the practice of the early church, since there is no reference in the gospels that Jesus ever used oil in healing. See James 5:14–16 for a later New Testament reference to the use of oil in healing.

[7] Mk 9:14–29; see Chapter 3.

[8] For a good discussion of healing from this perspective see John A. Sanford's *Healing and Wholeness.*

[9] Günther Bornkamn, *Jesus of Nazareth,* Chapter 9.

[10] My thanks to the Rev. Jerry Drino of San Jose, California, for this insight.

[11] See C.G. Jung, "Introduction to the Religious and Psychological Problems of Alchemy," *Psychology and Alchemy,* CW, Vol. 12, pp. 1–37.

[12] John A. Sanford, *Evil: The Shadow Side of Reality* and *The Strange Trial of Mr. Hyde: A New Look at the Nature of Human Evil.*

[13] See Chapter 5.

[14] The *Revised Standard Version* reads: "I wish those who unsettle you would mutilate themselves!" Other translations are more specific. *The New English Bible* has: "As for these agitators, they had better go the whole way and make eunuchs of themselves!" And the *Good News Bible* has: "I wish that the people who are upsetting you would go all the way; let them go on and castrate themselves!"

Chapter 13
Healing Today

Modern medicine comes down to us from Galen and Hippocrates, Greek physicians who were part of the ancient cult of Asklepios, the god of healing. According to myth, Asklepios, the son of Apollo, learned the healing arts from the centaur Chiron. He learned easily and became more skilled than his mentor, even succeeding in raising the dead. But this stirred the wrath of Hades, who complained to Zeus about the encroachment on his domain. Zeus responded by killing Asklepios. But after death Asklepios was given a place among the gods, from which, it was said, he effected even greater cures than before.

From Greece, the worship of Asklepios spread throughout the ancient world. More than four hundred temples were built from Egypt to Rome, with the most famous at Epidauros. The temples existed for one thousand years. Their disappearance coincided with the development of the healing shrines of the various saints the most recent example being that at Lourdes.

Clearly, then, modern medical science has religious roots. Today's surgery and pharmacology dominate a healing discipline that evolved from direct experience—usually through dreams—of the god of healing. Along with other aspects of ancient religions, the sacred practices of Asklepios were incorporated into Christianity. People began making pilgrimages to the gravesites of saints and martyrs associated with healing. As with Asklepios, the reports of healing became significantly more dramatic after the saints' death—when, presumably, they became channels of God's healing power.

Coincidentally, Christ's death and resurrection bear parallels to the story of Asklepios. Jesus also raised the dead, and in John's gospel he meets his own death after the raising of Lazarus. Afterward he ascends to heaven, taking his place with God. Then he emerges to dispense divine grace and healing.

In the absence of a gravesite for Christ, the graves of certain saints became the precincts where one could seek healing from God. As such sites proliferated and Christianity came to dominate the Mediterranean world, the temples of Asklepios yielded their place. Medieval physicians continued the medical science begun by Galen and Hippocrates and originally inspired by the Greek god of healing.

During the renaissance and the age of enlightenment, the scientific side of medicine began to grow, while the spiritual side declined. Healing was seen more and more in concrete, biological terms: illness was physiologically caused and could be remedied through medicine or surgery. By the end of the nineteenth century this became the exclusive view.

Early in the twentieth century, significant challenges to this approach began to emerge. As physicians studied certain cases more closely, they realized that some physical symptoms had emotional and psychological causes. Such cases gave impetus to Freud, Jung, and other early depth psychologists. A purely biological view of illness, they saw, was not enough—psychological and spiritual factors were also significant. With depth psychology and psychosomatic medicine, medical practice has been returning to its origins in the cult of Asklepios.[1]

According to Greek myth, Asklepios had two sons, Machaon and Podaleirios. Machaon was the first surgeon, while Podaleirios healed "invisible" ills, including those of the soul.[2] The work of Machaon has developed into today's medical practice. That of Podaleirios was absorbed into the healing cults of the saints and has gradually died out. It has so thoroughly disappeared from our religious institutions that the quest for meaning and the religious nature of the psyche frequently turn up in the psychotherapist's office. The loss from our churches of what Podaleirios represented is felt both inside and outside organized religion.

Depth psychology allows the forgotten side of the Greek god of healing to be recovered. Inner experiences crucial to healing become available once more. However, it offers more than a recovery of the healing of Asklepios; it opens the door for a recovery of the healing work of Jesus. Like the cult of Asklepios, Jesus' healing reflects the profound importance of spiritual and psychological elements. But while Asklepios, and the Christian cults that followed him, focused on the divine physician or god of healing, Jesus also stressed human interaction and human feeling. He carried on aspects of the ancient traditions of the shamans, human beings with healing personalities.[3] While linked to shamanism, Jesus also prefigures depth psychology. In a sense he was the first depth psychologist, preceding Freud and Jung by nineteen hundred years.

As we have seen, the healing that Jesus practiced and tried to pass on became lost as his divinity was proclaimed. Legends grew up around him after his death—the healing cult of the proclaimed divinity—but the fully human healer disappeared. Depth psychology allows us to renew not only the ancient religious roots of the physician, but also the shamanistic style of healing—in which the psyche lives fully in the interaction between two people.

The future of the church hinges on its capacity to integrate such healing into its life. The growing numbers who journey to the psychothera-pist's office nowadays demonstrate the desire and need for this. The church's recovery of healing in the decades ahead will go a long way in determining whether it answers Jesus' call, or whether the task will be left to others.

NOTES

[1] C.A. Meier, *Ancient Incubation and Modern Psychotherapy.*

[2] C. Kerenyi, *Asklepios: Archetypal Image of the Physician's Existence.*

[3] John A. Sanford, *Healing and Wholeness.* Chapter 3, "The Divine Physician," and Chapter 4, "The Ecstatic Healer," amplify some of the differences between the inner divine healer and the shamanistic healer.

Bibliography

Aland, Kurt, ed. *Synopsis of the Four Gospels.* Stuttgart: United Bible Societies, 1972.

Blatty, William Peter. *The Exorcist.* New York: Bantam Books, 1972.

Bolen, Jean Shinoda. *Goddesses in Everywoman: A New Psychology of Women.* San Francisco: Harper & Row, 1984.

Bornkamm, Günther. *Jesus of Nazareth.* New York: Harper & Row, 1960.

Borsch, Frederick Houk. *The Son of Man in Myth and History.* Philadelphia: Westminister Press, 1967.

The Boston Women's Health Book Collective. *Our Bodies, Ourselves.* New York: Simon and Schuster, 1973.

Burhmann, M. Vera. *Living in Two Worlds: Communication Between a White Healer and Her Black Counterparts.* Wilmette, Illinois: Chiron Publications, 1986.

Castaneda, Carlos. *A Separate Reality.* New York: Pocket Books, 1971.

———. *The Teachings of Don Juan: A Yaqui Way of Knowledge.* New York: Ballantine Books, 1968.

Castillejo, Irene de. *Knowing Woman.* New York: G.P. Putnam's Sons, 1973.

Christ, Carol P., and Judith Plaskow. *Womanspirit Rising: A Feminist Reader in Religion.* San Francisco: Harper & Row, 1979.

Cousins, Norman. *The Anatomy of an Illness.* New York: W.W. Norton, 1979.

Edinger, Edward F. *Ego and Archetype.* New York: G.P. Putnam's Sons, 1972.

Eliade, Mircea. *Rites and Symbols of Initiations: The Mysteries of Birth and Rebirth.* New York: Harper Torchbooks, 1958.

———. *Shamanism: Archaic Techniques of Ecstasy.* Princeton: Princeton University Press, 1964.

Evans, Elida. *A Psychological Study of Cancer.* New York: Dodd, Mead, & Company, 1926.

Frank, Jerome D. "The Medical Power of Faith." *Human Nature,* vol. 1, no. 8, 1978.

———. *Persuasion and Healing.* New York: Schocken Books, 1974.

Goldenberg, Naomi R. *Changing of the Gods: Feminism and the End of Traditional Religions.* Boston: Beacon Press, 1979.

Good News Bible. New York: American Bible Society, 1976.

Guggenbühl-Craig, Adolf. "The Archetype of the Invalid and the Limits of Healing." *Spring: An Annual of Archetypal Psychology and Jungian Thought,* 1979.

———. *Power in the Helping Professions.* New York: Spring Publications, 1971.

Harrison, R.K. "Disease" and "Healing," articles in *The Interpreter's Dictionary of the Bible.* Nashville: Abingdon Press, 1962.

Hillman, James, and Marie-Louise von Franz. *Jung's Typology.* New York: Spring Publications, 1971.

Jeremias, Joachim. *The Parables of Jesus.* New York: Charles Scribner's Sons, 1972.

John of the Cross. *The Dark Night of the Soul.* Garden City, N.Y.: Image Books, 1974.

Johnson, Robert. *He.* New York: Harper & Row, 1974, 1986.

Jung, C.G. *The Collected Works.* 20 vols. Princeton: Princeton University Press, 1953–79.

———. *Man and His Symbols.* New York: Doubleday, 1964.

———. *Memories, Dreams, Reflections.* New York: Pantheon Books, 1973.

———. *Modern Man in Search of a Soul.* New York: Harcourt, Brace & World, 1933.

Kapacinskas, Thomas J. "*The Exorcist* and the Spiritual Problem of Modern Woman." *Psychological Perspectives,* vol. 6, no. 2, 1975.

Kelsey, Morton T. *Afterlife: The Other Side of Dying.* New York: Paulist Press, 1979.

———. *Christianity and Healing.* New York: Harper & Row, 1973.

———. *Encounter with God.* Minneapolis: Bethany Fellowship, 1972.

———. *God, Dreams, and Revelation.* Minneapolis: Augsburg Publishing House, 1974.

Kerenyi, Carl. *Asklepios: Archetypal Image of the Physician's Existence.* New York: Pantheon Books, 1959.

Kreinheder, Albert. "The Healing Power of Illness." *Psychological Perspectives,* vol. 11, no. 1, 1980.

Kübler-Ross, Elisabeth. *Death: The Final Stage of Growth.* Englewood Cliffs, N.J.: Prentice-Hall, 1975.

———. *On Death and Dying.* New York: Macmillan, 1969.

Lame Deer, John Fire, and Richard Erdoes. *Lame Dear, Seeker of Visions.* New York: Simon and Schuster, 1972.

Lynch, James. *The Broken Heart.* New York: Basic Books, 1977.

Mahdi, Louise Carus, Steven Foster & Meredith Little. *Betwixt & Between:*

Patterns of Masculine and Feminine Initiation. LaSalle, Illinois: Open Court, 1987.

Meier, C.A. *Ancient Incubation and Modern Psychotherapy.* Evanston, Ill: Northwestern University Press, 1967.

Moody, Raymond, Jr. *Life After Life.* St. Simons Island, Ga.: Mockingbird Books, 1977.

————. *Reflections on Life After Life.* Covington, Ga.: Mockingbird Books, 1977.

The New English Bible. New York: Oxford University Press, 1976.

The New Oxford Annotated Bible (Revised Standard Version). New York: Oxford University Press, 1973.

Newcomb, Franc. *Hosteen Klah: Navajo Medicine Man and Sand Painter.* Norman, Okla.: University of Oklahoma Press, 1964.

Niehardt, John G. *Black Elk Speaks.* Lincoln: University of Nebraska Press, 1961.

Parvati, Jeannine. *Hygieia: A Woman's Herbal.* Berkeley, Cal.: Freestone Collective Books, 1978.

Pelgrin, Mark. *And a Time to Die.* Wharton, Ill.: Theosophical Publishing House, 1962.

Pelletier, Kenneth R. *Mind as Healer, Mind as Slayer.* New York: Delta Books, 1977.

Perrin, Norman. *Rediscovering the Teachings of Jesus.* New York: Harper & Row, 1967.

Perry, John W. *The Far Side of Madness.* Englewood Cliffs, N.J.: Prentice-Hall, 1974.

Power, Marla N. "Menstruation and Reproduction: An Oglala Case." *Signs: Journal of Women in Culture and Society,* vol. 6, no. 1, 1980.

Sandner, Donald. *Navajo Symbols of Healing.* New York: Harcourt Brace Jovanovich, 1979.

Sanford, Agnes. *The Healing Light.* St. Paul, Minn.: Macalester Park Publishing, 1947.

Sanford, John A. *Dreams and Healing.* New York: Paulist Press, 1978.

————. *Dreams: God's Forgotten Language.* Philadelphia: J.B. Lippincott, 1968.

————. *Evil: The Shadow Side of Reality.* New York: Crossroad Publishing, 1981.

————. *Fritz Kunkel: Selected Writings.* New York: Paulist Press, 1984.

————. *Healing and Wholeness.* New York: Paulist Press, 1977.

———. "Interview with John Sanford" with Phyllis Mather Rice. *Your Church,* January/February, 1980.

———. *The Kingdom Within: A Study of the Inner Meaning of Jesus' Sayings.* San Francisco: Harper & Row, 1987.

———. *The Man Who Wrestled with God.* New York: Paulist Press, 1974, 1983.

———. *The Strange Trial of Mr. Hyde: A New Look at the Nature of Human Evil.* San Francisco: Harper & Row, 1987.

Selye, Hans. *The Stress of Life.* New York: McGraw-Hill, 1976.

Siegel, Bernie S. *Love, Medicine & Miracles: Lessons Learned About Self-Healing from a Surgeon's Experience with Exceptional Patients.* New York: Harper & Row, 1986.

Simonton, O. Carl, Stephanie Mathews-Simonton, James Creighton. *Getting Well Again.* Los Angeles: J.P. Tarcher, 1978.

Throckmorton, Burton, H., Jr., ed. *Gospel Parallels.* Nashville: Thomas Nelson, 1967.

van der Post, Laurens. *The Heart of the Hunter.* New York: William Morrow, 1961.

von Franz, Marie-Louise, and James Hillman. *Jung's Typology.* New York: Spring Publications, 1971.

Watson, Lyall. *Lightning Bird.* New York: Simon and Schuster, 1982.

Webster, Douglas. "What Is Spiritual Healing?" Cincinnati: Forward Movement, n.d.

Wheelright, Jane Hollister. *The Death of a Woman.* New York: St. Martin's Press, 1981.

Wickes, Frances. *The Inner World of Childhood.* New York: Signet Books, 1968.

Woodman, Marion. *Addiction to Perfection: The Still Unravished Bride.* Toronto: Inner City Books, 1982.

———. *The Owl Was a Baker's Daughter: Obesity, Anorexia Nervosa, and the Repressed Feminine.* Toronto: Inner City Books, 1980.